MacPherson
Other Tales of the

MacPherson's Rant and Other Tales of the Scottish Fiddle

by

Stuart McHardy

Birlinn

First published in Great Britain in 2004 by
Birlinn Ltd
West Newington House
10 Newington Road
Edinburgh

www.birlinn.co.uk

ISBN 1 84158 290 5

British Library Cataloguing-in-Publication Data
A catalogue record for this book is available on request
from the British Library

Typeset by Initial Typesetting Services, Edinburgh
Printed and bound by
MPG Books Limited, Bodmin

Contents

Acknowledgements

I would like to thank Dr Sheila Douglas and Colin Douglas for their help in putting this book together.

Introduction

The Fiddle

The role of the fiddle in Scotland is a long and chequered one. As far back as the medieval period there were stringed instruments played with a bow, such as the croud mentioned in the fourteenth-century poem *Orfeo and Heurodis*. The croud was an early form of the fiddle, with a shallow rectangular body about sixty centimetres by thirty centimetres and five centimetres deep; it was probably the direct ancestor of the traditional box fiddle that survived into the twentieth century. Originally it had two horsehair strings, which were bowed, but later it developed three and six-string versions. It is quite likely that the fiddle developed independently in Scotland, though there were similar instruments in the Baltic countries of Estonia and Finland at an early date. They, like the croud, were probably of a tenor pitch. A similar instrument, the crwth, was still in use in Wales in the nineteenth century. It had four strings for bowing and two which could be bowed or plucked, set to one side of the fingerboard. Another version of the same instrument was the Shetland gue and it has been suggested that the instrument originally either came from the British Isles or Scandinavia. The long-term contacts between the peoples of these two areas make it impossible to be precise about such matters, as there has not been a great deal of investigation into the mutual influence between the peoples of Scandinavia and what we now call Scotland.

Another early bowed instrument was the rebec and there is a carving of one on the twelfth-century Melrose Abbey. Arguments have been put forward that such stringed instruments were brought back from the Crusades, which lasted from the eleventh to the thirteenth centuries. It seems more likely such stringed instruments were developed here in Scotland, or the British Isles. Similarities between the Shetland gue, the Welsh crwth and the bowed harp of Scandinavia make it impossible to decide in which direction influence travelled, so we might as well say that the fiddle is a truly Scottish instrument, as well as being indigenous to many other countries. What underlines its role as a native instrument is the music played on it and, as we shall see, in this respect Scottish music is distinctive. The name fiddle itself may have derived from an early Irish term 'fidil', but again it is impossible to be definitive about this.

What we can be absolutely sure of is the importance of the fiddle in Scottish music. There is the report of a French soldier and historian who visited Mary Queen of Scots in 1561 which tells of five or six hundred fiddlers coming to Holyrood to play for the queen. These were not professional musicians but citizens of Edinburgh. It is telling that John Knox, often portrayed as the personification of Puritanism, wrote positively about the same event. The instruments they were playing were most likely flat-topped, like rebecs. The arch-top of the modern fiddle came about through the influence of viols, which generally had six strings but were bowed like the fiddle. These instruments were brought in from the Continent in the sixteenth century and were very popular at the court. The improved construction, volume and tone of these instruments had a profound effect on indigenous instruments and the development towards what we now think of as the traditional fiddle was given a significant boost. It is reported that viols were played at the Cross in Edinburgh on the occasion of the coronation of James V in 1513. A considerable amount of music was written for these instruments, which were usually grouped in sixes with two each of the bass, tenor and treble instruments. Although the music for these instruments cannot really be considered as traditional or folk music, it is part of the development of Scottish music as a whole. The cross-fertilisation of musical styles between high art and traditional art is something that has always taken place; but amongst those more concerned with the high art end of the spectrum such mutual interplay is generally ignored, or at best under-rated. This tends to be more the result of social prejudice rather than any meaningful divergence in the different types of music.

A poem attributed to Thomas the Rhymer, who is said to have lived in the thirteenth century, tells of:

> Harp and fedyl both he fande
> The getern and the sawtry
> Lut and rybid ther gon gan'
> Thair was al maner of mynstralsy.

Sir Walter Scott, *Minstrelsy of the Scottish Border*,
vol IV, 1833 ed., Appendix

Here the getern probably refers to an early form of English guitar or a cithern; the sawtry is the psaltery and the rybid the rebec. The fiddle is just one of the portable musical instruments mentioned in the poem, but over the centuries its popularity has in no way diminished, while the others have disappeared. There are those who contend that the guitar developed independently in the British Isles and there is no doubt that there were what are now called 'English' guitars being made here in the seventeenth century and probably earlier. There was a substantial repertoire of tunes for the guitar and the lute in eighteenth-century Scotland, but, like some other instruments, their popularity faded away in the face of the widespread use of the fiddle. By the time the modern violin was finally developed in Italy in the seventeenth century by the Amati family, there was a ready audience for it all over Europe. Scotland was no exception; soon fiddle-makers in Scotland were using the new techniques and the indigenous tradition of fiddle-making was well established. Scotland may not have given birth to a Stradavarius or Guarneri but there are many fine old instruments that still repay the love and attention paid to them.

Collections of Scottish music began to be published from the late seventeenth century onwards but specific collections of fiddle tunes did not appear till the mid-eighteenth century. This is still earlier than the collections of tunes for Scotland's other main popular traditional instrument: the Highland bagpipe. The role of the pipes in Highland culture made them dubious in the eyes of many after the civil wars of the eighteenth century, even though pipes had actually been popular for a long time in many Lowland areas. The first collection of indigenous fiddle music was published in 1757, when Scots reels or country dances was published in Edinburgh. However, there are many extant copies of fiddlers' manuscripts from even earlier. It was common practice for fiddlers to keep their repertoires in manuscript form. Many of these contain quite a variety of tunes, such as jigs and reels, now historical forms such as bourrees and chaconnes, reflecting French influence, as well as slow airs. By the late eighteenth century collections like that of Angus Cumming, published in 1780, show us a vibrant and popular tradition of traditional music, much of it used to accompany dancing, an activity that was embraced by all classes of society. Although many collections of fiddle tunes were subsequently published, the line between composing specific melodies and developing tunes from traditional music is one that at times is indistinct.

The fiddle has been at the heart of all kinds of social activity in Scotland for hundreds of years. Its portability, volume and range made it an ideal instrument to be played at weddings, dances and all kinds of small-scale gatherings, within families or in public places. Its usefulness for dance music, as the accompaniment to singing and also its solo playing have made it an integral part of traditional music in Scotland. Its versatility has ensured that many traditional Scottish fiddlers have also played other types of music from classical to jazz.

Shetland

To the north of Scotland are the Orkney and Shetland Isles, both of which were for a long time part of the possessions of the Norwegian Crown. The Shetland Isles are the most northerly outpost of the United Kingdom – over a hundred low-lying and virtually treeless islands cluster together about as far from Aberdeen as the Faeroe Isles or Bergen on the west coast of Norway. Shetlanders often maintain that they are no more Scottish than Scandinavian. The Shetlands were ruled from Norway until 1469, and remnants of the old affiliations remain. To this day the dialect of Shetland is very distinct from other Scots dialects, reflecting its origins in Norn, the old local dialect of Norwegian. Shetland men, like many other Scottish islanders, have long been sea travellers; musically, they have always been open to outside influence, while still maintaining local traditions.

The fiddle in particular had long had a central place in Shetland culture. Even today the most famous proponent of the Shetland style of fiddle, Aly Bain, travels the world, and the instrument retains its popularity amongst Shetland's youngsters. The Shetland fiddle tradition is very much alive and well, preserving a continuity of traditional music that is hundreds of years old. The survival and growth of interest in the tradition was greatly encouraged by the late Tom Anderson in the twentieth century; under his influence, fiddle teaching became a regular part of the school curriculum in Shetland.

The development of the fiddle in Shetland has a unique history. At the turn of the nineteenth century, Sir Arthur Edmonstone wrote that around ten per cent of the Shetlanders played the violin and that at least some of the music was of Norse origin. He also mentioned the gue, an instrument with two horsehair strings that was played upright like a cello. Researchers have noted that this is something like an instrument from Iceland known as a fidla, and resemblances have also been noted with what has been called the Eskimo violin or 'tautirut', though both of these have also been referred to as bowed box-zithers. Whenever the violin actually arrived in Shetland, it is clear that it was absorbed into an indigenous and thriving string-playing tradition. In the 1970s a rough headcount of musicians was taken in the village of Cullivoe on the island of Yell. Of the seventy adult men, more than twenty were, or had been, fiddlers; guitars and accordions or melodeons were played by another nine. In addition, there were a further eight known to be singers, meaning that more than half the male adult community were musicians of one standard or another. Since then, of course, the fiddle has been taken up by more and more women, some of whom have achieved considerable professional success, and it is fair to say that the Shetland fiddle tradition continues to thrive into the twenty-first century.

Although there was no early history of violin-making in the islands, the tradition of Shetland men going off to sea – in the British navy and in the fishing and trading fleets of Britain, the Netherlands and Norway – meant there were always fiddles being brought back from elsewhere.

The role of the fiddle in Shetland was absolutely central in a variety of social rituals. These included weddings and the annual celebrations of Yule, during both of which the ancient tradition of guising also played a part. Guisers were groups of young men, dressed in truly ancient traditional clothes made primarily of straw, with high hats and blue veils over their faces, whose identity was always secret but without whose blessing many social occasions were considered incomplete, or worse. At weddings the 'scuddler' or chief guiser would lead off the dancing with the bride, while his companions danced with the other females of the wedding party. They would then be given a drink, after which they would leave and the general festivities would begin. One of the surviving auld or muckle reels that hark back to the days when Shetland was part of Norway is itself known as the Guisers' Reel.

Dancing in Shetland had its own traditions too, some of which, like guising, seem to hark back to ancient times indeed. Some of the tunes survive in fragments known as the 'Auld Reels' or 'Muckle Reels'. While it is clear that the old style was affected by incoming tunes from the mainland of Scotland, brought in by both Scottish farm workers and the fishermen who came to Shetland's shores every year, the Shetland tradition remains distinctive. Though today the majority of tunes surviving in Shetland can be seen as part of the wider Scottish fiddle tradition.

A great deal of literature has been written about Shetland folklore, in which the fiddle played a central part, and it is clear that fiddlers have always had a respected role in island society. Descriptions of early weddings and dances all note the importance of the fiddler. They also had a role to play on ships, particularly during the nineteenth-century flourishing of the whaling industry. It was not unusual for whaling ships to be caught in the winter ice and forced to overwinter in the darkness of the far north. The presence of a Shetland fiddler or two amongst the crew would be a great advantage in staving off the boredom and monotony of the months spent in virtually permanent darkness. In fact, every Shetland ship would have at least one fiddle. Ships from other areas would have melodeon players or fiddlers. All were hired either as common sailors or specialists, such as carpenters, but their musical abilities entitled them to an extra share of the eventual catch.

The Fiddle and the Dance

The fiddle has long been central to the Scottish dance tradition even though, like all musical instruments, it was anathema to the more extreme Presbyterians of the period immediately after the Reformation. This period actually saw the prohibition of dancing and widespread denunciation from the pulpit of all sorts of normal human activities – in Scotland we have historically had a lot of problems arising from religious differences. The Protestant Reformers of the sixteenth century seem to have been particularly incensed by the dances that took place at the Scottish court. Queen Mary brought back many new dances from France and some of these were considered almost obscene. That France was a Catholic country and the Reformers were of a puritanical Protestant bent just made the situation worse. This antagonistic attitude survived into the seventeenth century, with people regularly being hauled before Kirk Session and fined or otherwise punished for dancing. The fact that there are so many references to this from the period shows that the prohibition on dancing never really worked – it was too much part of contemporary culture to be eradicated completely. As late as 1668 a farmer in North Knapdale was refused a certificate of church membership because he practised dancing. Thankfully, he had the decision overthrown on appeal and we hear no more of this ridiculous prohibition, despite the minister concerned claiming that dancing 'was a sin and bitter provocation to the Lord'.

Many eighteenth-century fiddlers continued the tradition of accompanying dancing – some fiddlers made a living as dancing masters and many of them toured the country instructing and playing for dances. The dances that took place ranged from those held in threshing barns on farmtouns to great society balls in Edinburgh, Glasgow and elsewhere – and all of them needed fiddlers. The farmtouns were where much of Scotland's rural population lived until the eighteenth century. People farmed rented lands in common, using the ancient runrig system. These cottars, as they were known, suffered the same fate as so many of their Highland cousins later did – they were cleared from the land as soon as the landowners came up with a way of making more ready cash through 'agricultural improvement'. As with all traditional music forms, there were also a great many people who played for their own amusement; though many of them wanted to 'make the big time' and become dancing masters themselves.

Auld Clootie and the Fiddle

During the tragic years of witch persecutions in Scotland, many women were burnt at the stake. Their execution usually followed their confession of their supposed evil deeds. The fact that these confessions were extracted by torture was in no way seen as diminishing their force and relevance. After all, hadn't they been accused of being witches? Not only is the barbaric and mis-ogynistic treatment of these women a foul blot on Scotland's history, the confessions themselves seem to have been put in the women's mouths. Time and again we hear the same things being confessed in virtually the same words. While there were un-doubtedly some pagan cult activities surviving into the eighteenth century and later, the behaviour that the witches confessed to were more to do with the expectations of the people torturing them than with reality.

Time and again they confessed to having consorted with Satan and of dancing regularly at witches' covens. The dances were rarely described in detail, but were assumed to be orgiastic. And time and again we find that the music for such dancing was said to have been provided by the devil himself. His preferred instru-ments were the fiddle and the bagpipes, the most popular instruments in Scotland throughout the seventeenth and eighteenth centuries. The best description of this fantasy occurs in Burns's 'Tam o Shanter', where Auld Clootie is playing the pipes. But in many other instances he is portrayed as playing the fiddle. We must remember that for many of the fanatically puritanical clergy of Scotland in the years following 1560 all music other than hymns and psalms were the devil's work. Dancing too was seen as essentially sinful in anything other than strictly controlled gatherings. Burns satirised such notions in the song 'The Deil's Awa wi the Exciseman', in which Auld Hornie 'cam fiddlin thru the toun, and danced awa with Exciseman.' Popular opinion of the exciseman made it likely that his idea of the devil taking away 'gaugers', as they were known, was widely appreciated. Although Burns himself worked as an exciseman, his basic beliefs regarding the taxation on spirits are probably summed up in the phrase 'Whisky an Freedom gang thegither.' It is notable that the devil in Scotland, sitting playing the fiddle or the pipes, bears little resemblance to the epitome of evil as represented by Satan, the fallen angel in charge of the fires of hell.

But the idea of the devil fiddling for the witches was a strong one, reinforced by the words put in the mouths of many so-called witches by their persecutors in the horrendous witch trials of the sixteenth and seventeenth centuries. Time after time in the heart-rending reports of such trials we clearly see that the poor victims were brutally and systematically tortured till they told their persecutors exactly what they wanted to hear. The idea of the satanic musician crops up in some odd ways, perhaps none more so than the placename Fiddlenaked Park in Airdrie. Local tradition tells us it was the rendezvous of wizards and witches, who met to celebrate their unholy Sabbats. They were said to have danced naked round their fiddler, who was also unclothed and may or may not have been Auld Clootie himself. It was generally a place that people reckoned was best avoided after dark. When we remember that traditional tales tell of public rituals in which young couples made love in stone circles at midsummer, it is conceivable that such remnants are in fact faint echoes of ancient religious practice from pagan times.

Even today people sometimes try to use what they think is magic. A couple of hundred years ago such practices were much more widespread. There were, for instance, widespread practices of divination – trying to see into the future – which took place at Halloween. These are relatively well known and many of them are described in Robert Burns' poem 'Halloween'. Some people think that 'dookin for apples' is a remnant of an ancient ritual of looking into the future. However, there were lots of other practices that were common when most of the population of Scotland still lived in rural areas. Many rituals, such as visiting healing wells, involved doing certain things a specific number of times. After making a prayer, it was common to have to go round such wells three or even nine times to make sure that the prayer worked. While many such rituals were basically concerned with healing, in days when going to the doctor was too expensive for many poor people, there were other types of magic practice that were resorted to.

While Christian ministers often saw such types of behaviour as little different from Black Magic, or seeking help directly from the devil, it is much more likely that they are remnants of practices that were common in pagan times. The idea that people worshipped the devil before the enlightenment of Christianity came upon them is erroneous. The truth is that long after Christianity came to the British Isles people continued to carry out 'superstitious' practices out of sight of the priests and ministers, mainly because they thought that such activities worked. Their parents and grandparents had done such things and it was better to be safe than sorry; so they kept up the practices.

One of the stranger beliefs was that if you crawled underneath a brier rose or bramble that was rooted in the earth at both ends your wishes would be granted. To make this charm or spell work it was necessary to crawl under it, naked, nine times in all. Such rites would usually be carried out on the ancient holy days of

Beltane, 1 May, or Samhain, 1 November, which were the most magical days in the old pagan year.

The Role of Storytelling

The material in this book is taken from both traditional tales and reminiscences, and memoirs of actual events. Recent research has shown that the oral tradition, long spurned by historians as little more than entertainment, does in fact contain memories of events and societies that can help us gain a clearer picture of how people lived in the past. Many such stories have survived over remarkable periods of time and have eventually been written down in collections. Though some such stories may come from the twentieth century, others have roots that are hundreds or even thousands of years old. While historians prefer to rely on the written word to tell us of our past, we are only now becoming aware that the oral tradition can in fact retain factual data over thousands of years. Stories have been told for as long as people have been on the planet and the process of storytelling was how knowledge was passed on from generation to generation, whether it was practical knowledge, mythology and ritual, or tales of heroes and heroines. Such tales continue to be told for as long as the audience finds them relevant and are not necessarily super-seded by the arrival of literacy. There is currently a worldwide surge of interest in storytelling and we are only now beginning to understand that these remnants of the past can teach us a great deal about our ancestors. We should remember that even in the modern Western world not everyone can read and write.

Just a couple of hundred years ago literacy was often very limited amongst the rural and urban working classes. So, although the storytelling tradition was not as structured as it had been in earlier times, it continued to flourish. Even today you hear people in pubs, at parties and other social gatherings who are natural storytellers; often the stories they tell are based on traditional material – old tales in new clothes. The historians' obsession with paper and dates has blinded us to the fact that oral transmission retains a great deal of information about what life for our ancestors was like, and about how they saw the world they inhabited.

The fact that such fiddle tales occur in many different places tells us something more about the process of storytelling. In order to have the maximum impact – and particularly to ensure that children would understand the stories – the locale of all different types of story motif would be presented as immediately local to the audience. There would be little point in talking of far-off places that few if any of the audience would ever visit. This is why so many versions of significant tales, including those of 'King Arthur', can be found in so many different places. Such local variants do not have to stem from one original location, though they might possibly do so. Within the culture of the local group, reliant on oral transmission and memory to survive, stories, whether legendary or mythological, would always tend to be set in the local landscape.

This is something that is only now beginning to be truly understood – in the past the similarity of a story told in Scotland to one from England or even Greece was usually accounted for by the story being imported. Probably the clearest example of this is the existence of Arthurian material in both placename and story in different parts of Scotland. This has been explained in the past as having come about because of the literary influence of the works of Geoffrey of Monmouth, the twelfth-century monk who popularised Arthurian stories in his *History of the Kings of Britain* and the *Life of Merlin*. This has been accepted by historians without question, but ignores the fact that story survives longest amongst people who are the last to acquire literacy and are thus least influenced by it. Popular culture has always had a strong oral element and there are areas of overlap in both theme and presentation between story, song and music.

Even into the twentieth century, many of the travelling people of Scotland were brought up within a culture that was still essentially oral-based, despite the last few generations having become literate.

The same stories survive in different locales, languages and cultures because they speak to common human understanding. Although some stories, such as tales of extinct animals and cataclysmic geophysical events in Australia, have survived for tens of thousands of years, our stories of fiddlers are of course much more recent. They are, however, part of a continuum of tradition that is truly ancient, and in their presentation of human society and activity retain the capacity to speak to us.

As interest in storytelling grew in the years after the Second World War, the extent of the treasure that was contained in the traditional tales of Scotland's travelling people began to be understood. Some of the stories retold here are from that tradition, while others have been gleaned from local histories and literary collections. While much scholarship has concentrated on collecting tales from the lips of those travellers who still 'had' the stories, it has become clear that there are also many other stories hidden away in books. Other truly ancient stories survive in changed guise within urban traditions. Stories from the far distant past have survived alongside stories from more modern times and both types appear here. As our understanding of the value of the storytelling tradition and the material it has allowed to survive increases, we can perhaps begin to have a clearer idea of just what the past in Scotland was like. The historians tell us about the deeds of the 'high heid yins': kings and nobles, soldiers, religious leaders and the rich. The storytelling tradition reminds us that such material refers only to a tiny portion of human society at any one time.

In a fundamental sense, story tells us the true history of the people. And in Scotland the fiddle has always been important to the people playing it and the people listening to it, not just to the lairds who could afford to maintain professional musicians. Although we nowadays think of the professional musicians, fiddlers and pipers who attended clan chiefs as in some way the 'chief's' musicians, their true original role was more like what we would nowadays recognise as a community musician. They played for all the people of the clan, a term meaning children, which really describes Scottish tribes all claiming descent from a single common ancestor. Traditionally, the chiefs were not over the clan, but part of it. Their role was like that of the town fiddlers, who, like the town pipers, were a fixture in many Lowland Scottish towns.

Dr Samuel Johnson showed how story has been misunderstood when he wrote the following:

> Books are faithful repositories, which may be a while neglected or forgotten, but when they be are opened again, will impart their instruction: memory, once interrupted, is not to be recalled.

This is true, but ignores the role of oral transmission in many areas, including the British Isles – a role that still continues in a diminished form. Books are usually written by individuals and very often for pay. The repetition of traditional story within a closed social group is something completely different; its authenticity is a matter of importance for the entire group, and there would always be people of considerable knowledge other than the bard or seannachie telling the story. In fact, the same stories would have been told and retold and most, if not all, of the social group would have a considerable knowledge of them, making it virtually impossible to alter or distort the inherent matter of such stories. Like all artists, however, each storyteller would probably have his own way of presenting his tales. It was through story that children learned moral precepts, the history of their ancestors, how the world was made and many practical lessons. Although stories have always had to be entertaining – to ensure people paid attention – within societies dependent on oral transmission they were never just entertainment, and even today many storytellers' material has strong moral precepts. There is also the fact that story helps to teach the young about the world in which they live on many levels at once – the old notion that storytelling is a simple art form is not one which stands up to much scrutiny. Johnson's point that memory, once interrupted, is not to be recalled is true, but in Scotland we are in the very fortunate position that a great many traditional stories have been written down. And there are still stories being collected today that have survived through the process of oral transmission. In one sense, story itself is the point rather than the actual material of any particular tale – as long as people want to hear a particular story, and tell it among themselves, the psychological and social relevance of the tale will continue. History is certainly written by winners, but stories are told by history's survivors.

Language

Traditional stories in Scotland survive in three languages, English, Gaelic and Scots. The latter two languages have been in use here for at least 1,500 years, probably longer, while English as it is spoken today in Scotland has come in since the sixteenth century. Stories survive in the languages people use and no story is any more authentic than another merely by virtue of its language. There has been an unfortunate idea propagated over the last couple of centuries that Scots is a descendant of English and thus is less truly indigenous than Gaelic. In fact Scots comes from the same roots as English but developed separately from it.

Fechtin Fiddlers

⟫◦⟪

Even well into the eighteenth century there were many parts of Scotland where it was the norm for men to go around armed. Our history is one in which there have been long periods where the rule of law was little different from the rule of the sword. James MacPherson is probably the most famous of the fechtin fiddlers, but has been romanticised extensively. The indistinct figure of Rattlin Willie reminds us that for long enough the Borders of Scotland were just as wild as the Highlands, while the story of Johnny Faa has given rise to many songs of the Gypsy Davy style.

MacPherson's Rant

James MacPherson was a man who embodied much of the spirit of the Highland warrior; he is remembered to this day as a famous swordsman and noted fiddler. Born in the second half of the seventeenth century, he was the natural son of MacPherson of Invereshie and a tinker lass of the Broun family. James was raised in both families and inherited much from both. Although 'tinkers' became almost a term of insult for the travelling people of Scotland, they have never forgotten that they are the descendants of travelling metal-workers whose skills were valued by communities all across the country. Some of today's travellers suggest that they can trace their ancestry back to the original hunter-gatherers who came to Scotland when the Ice Age retreated, thousands upon thousands of years ago. Whatever the truth of that, the travelling people have a fierce pride in their own ancestry; James was probably as proud of his mother's people as his father's, and it is likely that his skill as a fiddler was learned among the former. His father, Invereshie – it was the norm for Scots to be called after the lands they owned, or worked – was a minor chieftain of the Clan MacPherson, and a man of some standing within the clan community. There was great emphasis on all the males being trained as warriors; this was in fact central to the social system of the Highland clans. James proved a ready pupil in this respect and developed into a fine swordsman. His preferred weapon was the claymore, the great double-handed sword of the Gael, and his own sword was of such size and weight that few could wield it with any skill.

In this period inter-clan raiding was rife; it was how the warriors proved their worth. When the harvest was in, groups of young, and not so young, clan warriors would set off by the light of the harvest moon to 'lift' the cattle of rival clans. For a long, long time the black cattle of the Highlands were how the Gaels judged wealth and success, and there was no greater feat than lifting the cattle of another clan. This was not rustling or theft, but the way of the warrior in a society that had probably changed little since the Iron Age. To Lowlanders the 'caterans' of the Highland areas seemed to be no more than thieves, but amongst the Gaels things were different. James was steeped in ancient tradition and clearly understood the ancient way of the cateran. However, even as far back as the seventeenth century the old ways were changing: more and more of the clan chiefs abandoned their traditional role as father of the tribe and began to become little more than large landowners, obsessed with personal wealth. As the Lowland areas began to develop their agriculture and the old ways of barter gave way to a modern money-based economy, the differences between the people farming the fertile lands adjoining the Highlands and the fierce proud people of the mountains grew greater. In the

Lowland areas law was a matter for local judges, effectively answerable to the government in Edinburgh, while in the Highlands loyalty to clan and the power of the sword arm dominated. As the gulf between the societies grew, there were those of the Highland clans who increasingly saw their Lowland neighbours as fair game for raiding.

To the peaceful Lowlanders the Highlanders' obsession with arms and fighting, and with 'lifting' cattle, was utterly foreign. Although there were those who spoke both Gaelic, the Celtic language of the Highland clans, and Scots, the Germanic tongue of the Lowland peoples, the cultural and language differences made the two communities increasingly alien to each other. It is hardly surprising in this situation that people in the Lowland areas came to see the Highland raiders as nothing more than thieves; there were many in both camps who had nothing but contempt for the other side. What was honourable to one side was criminal to the other and there were those in the Highlands who took advantage of the situation and lived off raiding alone.

James was a man who loved the outdoor life and spent many a night on the hill listening to the age-old stories of Finn MacCoul and his warriors, the Fianna, as they hunted and raided. Central to the belief of the Highland warrior was *cothrom no Feinne*, the fair play of the Fianna, a code of honour that had developed over the centuries. Traditionally, clans would never raid their neighbours, as this would lead to permanent warfare; so they often travelled long distances to lift cattle.

While James and his companions, some of whom were his cousins on his mother's side, saw themselves as behaving like warriors, by the farmers and lairds they raided in the Lowland areas of Moray, Buchan and Aberdeenshire they were seen as a curse. The differences between the increasingly modern economy in the Lowland areas and the ancient warrior society of the Highland clans were bound to lead to problems. With the additional problems of clan feuds and personal enmity between fierce and proud warriors, it is clear that James lived in dangerous and volatile times.

The first we hear of him is when he was arrested for theft and found guilty at a court in Aberdeen. He had been betrayed and, as a Highland cateran in a Lowland court, he knew he had little chance of justice. His sentence was a foregone conclusion – death by hanging. However, James, as well as being a skilful warrior and a fine musician, was also known to have a way with the ladies and while he was in prison the serving maid of the magistrate who tried him took a fancy for the big, handsome Highlander. She herself had come from the Highlands and managed to get word to some of James's closest companions that he was due to be hanged in Aberdeen on a certain day. The gallows was just outside the tolbooth, the traditional prison of Scottish towns, and James could see it from the window of his prison, where he was kept in chains. He was due to be hanged at noon on a Saturday, when all the common people of the city would be there to see the end of this Highland thief, as the judge had called him. Among that crowd would be many who originally came from the Highland areas, and many more who had relatives there. They were poor people and had no cattle to be stolen; many of them sympathised with the handsome Highlander.

The day of the execution came and a good crowd had gathered. Executions were not that common and were seen by the magistrates as giving a lesson to the populace, while many of the common people saw such events as entertainment. Large crowds would gather and that would attract pedlars and per-formers, much like the country fairs of the day. Among the crowd were two of James's cousins, Donald MacPherson and Peter Broun, himself a noted fiddler. Donald was a giant, even by the standards of the Highlanders, and had been on many a raid with his cousin; Peter was himself a powerful, clever and nimble young man. An hour before the execution, the two men approached the tolbooth through the growing crowd. Up the stairs they went. Donald hammered on the tolbooth door with the pommel of his sword. Inside there was just one warder and, as he opened the door, Peter burst in. As the warder fell back, Donald came though the door and, with one blow from the hilt of his sword, laid the man out cold. Quick as a flash, Peter grabbed the keys from the man's belt and opened the cell door. There was no time to try and loosen James's chains, so Peter threw him over his shoulders and followed Donald back out of the door. Down the stairs of the tolbooth they went and a cheer went up from the crowd.

Not everyone in Aberdeen was sympathetic to the Highlander though. A local butcher, whose shop overlooked the tolbooth square, had suffered financially from raids by James and others and decided to intervene. He was as big as Donald and no coward. He had a great bulldog, which he commanded to attack Donald just as he reached the foot of the stairs. Donald was no fool. In a practised motion, he undid his belt and threw his plaid over the butcher. The dog, confused but smelling something strange, went for his master, pulling the unfortunate man to the ground. By now, some of the gathered crowd had cottoned on to what was happening and started a fight. Someone had sent for the town guard, but when they arrived the whole square was a seething, scrapping mass of humanity. Donald and Peter carried James through the crowd to where another of their band was waiting with horses in a side street. Unceremoniously, James was dumped over the back of a horse; the others mounted and off they rode. No one had a chance to tell the men on the city gates what was happening and the men of the town guard there could only jump aside as the Highlanders galloped through the city gate and off to their Highland retreat.

James returned to his cateran ways and his reputation increased. While this was perhaps to his advantage amongst the clansmen of Marr and Buchan, it caused even greater resentment in the Lowland areas of the northeast. He seems to have had the support of the laird of Grant, on whose lands he and his cousins, the Brouns, lived when not out raiding. Grant was keen to hold on to the old clan ways and considered all those who lived on his lands to be under his own jurisdiction. In an attempt to control the often bloody confrontations between raiding Highlanders and Lowland farmers, the government had given many clan chiefs legal control over their own clansmen, though they did not have supremacy over the established sheriff courts in the Lowland areas. The system had been out of use for twenty years, but Grant was still trying to control things as he had earlier.

A few years later, James, whose winning ways and popularity with the ladies caused some jealousy even among his own people, was once again betrayed. The laird of Braco, who was determined to put an end to the raiding, was informed that MacPherson and some of the Brouns were to be in attendance at the Summer's Eve Fair in Keith. Accordingly, he set out with his brother-in-law Lesmurdie and over a dozen hand-picked men. Sure enough, as they got to the fair there was MacPherson. The battle was short but desperate, one of MacPherson's band being killed outright. James and Peter were grabbed, along with Peter's brother and another band-member, James Gordon, while the rest of the caterans made their escape. The four of them were taken to a nearby house and a guard of half a dozen men was set around the house. Braco and Lesmurdie were sitting in an upstairs room of the house when they heard a commotion outside. This was the laird of Grant, who had turned up with thirty of his own men to set MacPherson free. Braco, realising the seriousness of the situation, came down the stairs and said to Grant, 'I had intended sending these men to prison, but that seems difficult now that you have arrived. There are too many of you to contend with, so I shall leave.'

Grant and his men stood aside to let Braco and his group go off, content that they had achieved their aim of freeing their friends. However, Braco, as soon as he was out of sight, headed back to the market and, finding two other justices of the peace there, soon rounded up sixty armed men. He then went hot-foot back to where he had left MacPherson and the laird of Grant. This time Grant was outnumbered – two to one – and, realising that there was no hope of victory, he went off leaving MacPherson and his companions to the mercy of Braco's men.

The trial took place before the sheriff in Banff in November 1700. James and his companions were charged with a variety of offences, including the wonderful-sounding 'masterful bangstrie and oppression' – which translates as something like extortion and grievous bodily harm. The laird of Grant had sent a lawyer, who pleaded to the court that as the accused were all from his lands they should be surrendered for trial to him. He also offered a pledge for their lawful behaviour, but the situation was too far gone and the trial went ahead. Witness after witness was called to testify that they had stolen sheep, cattle and horses, had broken into houses, had stolen people's purses and wallets, and generally oppressed many poor people in the area. They were said to have had their own language, probably a form of Romany cant, and to have spent many nights in debauchery and dancing, with MacPherson and Peter Broun providing the music on the fiddle. The verdict was a foregone conclusion and James and Peter Broun were sentenced to be hanged the next market-day, the following Saturday.

The time for the execution was set for one o'clock. The laird of Grant had many friends and was frantically trying to get a stay of execution from higher authorities in Aberdeen. In this he was successful, but it was a long way by horse from Aberdeen to Banff. The day of the execution came. At eleven o'clock James was told he was being hanged at twelve, not one o'clock. Somehow the sheriff had heard that a warrant to stay the execution was on its way from Aberdeen and that the bearer of the warrant was due at about half past twelve. James knew his time had come. His friend Grant would not be able to save him.

When he was led out to the scaffold he looked around the town square of the coastal town of Banff. There was no sympathy there. None of his friends had managed to get into the town and there was not a Highlander to be seen. The gathered people were townspeople and fishermen, people who saw him merely as a Highland thief. James asked for his fiddle, which he had had with him when captured. Then, before the crowd assembled to see his death, he played the tune he had composed while waiting in the cell to be hanged, the tune we now know as 'MacPherson's Rant'. There were many there who were impressed by the demeanour and courage of the big kilted Highlander standing on the scaffold, playing as always with style and verve.

When he finished, James held out his fiddle and asked, 'Who will take this fiddle from my hand? It is a good instrument and has many tunes left in it.'

His question was met with silence. No one wanted his fiddle. Looking round, he saw nothing but strange faces. He had no friends in the crowd. So, taking the fiddle in both his hands, he snapped the instrument over his knee, flung the pieces on the scaffold and went boldly to his death. Less than an hour later the rider from Aberdeen came to the square with a warrant for James's stay of execution, only to be met with the sight of the great Highland raider's body twisting on the end of a rope.

The pieces of the fiddle were gathered up and survive in the Clan MacPherson Museum in Newtonmore. The song itself, taken up and improved by Robert Burns, has remained popular to this day.

Rattlin Willie

Rattlin Willie is said to have been a fiddler in the Scottish Borders at the time when all men there went about armed. The tradition of the Border rievers (raiders), like that of the Highland clans, is best remembered for their habit of raiding rival families and Lowland farms. In both societies, the practice of raiding had possibly survived since ancient tribal times when all men were warriors. The fearsome reputation of the Border rievers spread throughout the adjoining areas of both Scotland and England. While the Highlands had their clans, the Borders had a plethora of families known for their prowess at arms and fearlessness. For generations Armstrongs, Elliots, Kerrs, Maxwells, Nixons and others held their lands on the border by force of arms, defying the kings of Scotland. Like their Highland cousins they were fond of hunting, but probably their favourite occupation was raiding. As in the Highlands, raids were considered to be most successful when little or no blood was shed but if somebody was killed while 'lifting' cattle a blood feud could very easily develop. It was into this warrior society, bound by ties of kinship rather than any feudal hierarchy, that Rattlin Willie was born.

Raised in Jedburgh, Willie was likely to have been a Home (pronounced Hume) or a Scott. Like all young men in the Borders, he would have been fiercely proud of his family name and aware of his kinship obligations to others of the same name. This also meant that people from other notable families were potential enemies. It is easy to imagine how young men raised to handle arms from an early age and steeped in the stories and traditions of their kin could be easily provoked to using their weapons. However, the use of arms wasn't the only manly attribute of the Border men. Just as the Norse Vikings loved to compose and hear poetry and the Highland warriors danced and played harps, the Borderers were fond of music. They had their own small bellows pipe and, of course, the fiddle.

In Willie's time a good bow arm was as well respected as a good sword arm, and he had a fine bow arm. His playing was of a high standard and, in a place like Jedburgh, it was inevitable that he would come into musical competition with other fiddlers.

It was just such a competition that was ultimately to bring about his end. One evening, he was playing in a local inn when another fiddler entered. He, like Willie, carried a sword on his back but a fiddle in his arms. He was Robin Elliot, a member of a family with whom Willie's people had often clashed over the years, but there in the tavern the matter was music, not old grudges. Elliot was a few years older than Willie, who was still in his early twenties, and had heard that there was a good young fiddler in the town. Being a keen musician himself, he had sought Rattlin Willie out. The two fiddlers played together for over an hour, sharing a drink or two as they played. Then matters took an ominous turn. They were playing an old Border dance tune in unison when Willie played it differently from Elliot. At once the older man stopped and said, 'That wisnae right there, lad.'

Willie was taken aback. 'Well, it's the way my uncle aye played it an it's the way we ken it in our family,' he replied a bit stiffly.

Now, it might have been the drink, or it might have been in Elliot's mind the whole time that he intended putting the younger man in his place.

'Well, maybe when you have been playin as long as me you'll learn the right way,' Elliot said, with a smile that had no humour or friendliness in it.

'Are you sayin you're a better fiddler than me?' asked Willie, ominously.

Now, Robin had heard that Willie was a fine fiddler and had been a bit taken aback to find the younger man was actually more of a player than himself. This was what was making him act in this way; but he hadn't heard that Willie was known for something else – his skill with any weapon.

By now both men had laid their fiddles down on the table they were sitting at.

'Well, I think that's obvious tae all here, don't you,' Elliot said, haughtily.

'No, I do not,' said Willie, standing up.

26

'Right then,' said Elliot, sure that he could outfight this young whippersnapper.

At this, the innkeeper ran over, shouting, 'Outside, outside. I want nae bather in here. Ye can baith jist get outside, right now.'

So out they went and the weapons that they had laid behind the door as they entered the tavern were taken up. Both men favoured the great two-handed broadsword that has figured so much in Scotland's history. They faced off and Elliot immediately sprang at Willie, swinging his great sword at the young man's head. Willie parried the stroke and thrust Robin back. All at once the older man realised that Willie might not look that strong but that he was extremely and deceptively powerful. Try as he might, Elliot couldn't land a blow on the youngster, who, he began to realise, was just biding his time. The result was a foregone conclusion to all who knew Willie. He simply waited till his man began to tire of swinging the great blade, then closed in for the kill. Once he went on the attack it was a matter of seconds before he caught the other fiddler a great blow on the side the head, killing him instantly.

It had been a fair fight and no one was going to bring any officers of the law into the affair. Robin Elliot had insulted Rattlin Willie and they had fought it out like men. In those days the rule of law was at best sporadic in the Borders and no one seemed too keen to try and bring Willie to book.

However, the other members of Robin's family were hardly likely to take the same attitude. They had lost one of their own and, in the code of the Border warrior, this called for some form of retribution, if not outright revenge. Willie knew fine well that the Elliots would come after him and he was ready for whatever came his way. He expected, however, that, just as he had fought fair with Robin, he would be challenged to fight one on one by some of Robin's relatives. This was his fatal mistake.

It was not long after his fight with Robin Elliot that Willie's bowing arm was stilled for good. He was ambushed by two of

Elliot's cousins and, despite his own skill, the two of them proved too much for him and killed him. The Borders had lost two fine fiddlers.

As Tam Cramb Would Say . . .

Tam Cramb the fiddler was a very well-known figure in southern Perthshire in the nineteenth century. A tall, powerful man with a thick and glossy beard of which he was particularly proud and which took great pleasure in grooming, Tam could, like many others of his time, turn his hand to a wide variety of jobs. Although a slater by trade, he took great delight in physical labour, particularly at hairst (harvest) time. He liked nothing better than to help stack the crops in farms up and down the length of the Carse of Gowrie. In those days much of the labour on farms and estates was still done by hand. Out in the fields at harvest-time, men took a pride in how many threaves – a threave was twenty-four separate sheaves – they could stack in a day. The competition would probably be a bit like that between sheep-shearers, with a lot of pride and a few side-bets riding on the result. This was hard physical work and, even after the development of farm machinery, the harvest remained a time of back-breaking work. Pitchforking wet bales of hay onto the back of flatbed trailers was rough work well into the 1970s in much of Scotland.

Tam was known for being able to stack between twenty and twenty-four threaves in a day's work – mind you in those days a day's work could easily be twelve hours of hard, back-breaking labour. Such demanding physical work was of great help to Tam in some of his activities – he was a noted performer as a heavy at the Highland Games, throwing weights, tossing the caber and so on. The phenomenon of the Highland Games was popular throughout the nineteenth century and, while today people know about the big events like the Braemar Gathering, in those far-off times there were many more games. The population of the countryside, given the extensive demand for physical labour in farming, was considerably more than it is today and this provided a ready audience. The most popular sports were always the heavy events. Even to this day there are many local games held around Scotland which make no attempt to attract tourists, retaining their essentially local character. Though today we would probably be surprised to find a Highland Heavy who was also a dancer and fiddler.

Tam, however, combined these abilities to good effect – he was fine dancer and a sought-after fiddler – more than just a fine physical specimen, though he surely was that and he knew it. Always well turned-out, he usually sported a tall hat and a frock coat and was known for his ready wit and confident way. In fact, he had a reputation as a man of wisdom. There were many who would precede a wise or witty saying with the phrase, 'As Tam Cramb would say . . .' He was, in short, a man of some standing in his community and as a fiddler and dancer was considered to be of the very first order. Combined with his undoubted capacity for hard work, this made him both well known and popular amongst the general populace. He was clearly a man who, despite his high opinion of his own abilities, retained the 'common touch'.

One day, Tam had arranged to meet with a group of his pals from Wolfhill, a Strathmore village in the shadow of Dunsinane Hill, where Shakespeare wrote that Macbeth was finally defeated. It is true that there was a fort on the top of the hill and that Macbeth used it. Tam and his friends had arranged to meet up in the Black Bull Inn at Perth. By the time he got there it was obvious that trouble was brewing. Words had been exchanged and the atmosphere between the regular 'townies' in the Black Bull and the visitors from Wolfhill was getting worse by the second. In those days brawls were hardly uncommon and there was often bad blood between the town and country people. Into the midst of this seething cauldron stepped the tall, imposing figure of Tam Cramb, his tall hat and full beard adding to the impression of size and strength. Immediately all eyes were upon him.

'Excuse my interference, gentlemen,' boomed the big man, 'but I perceive this is all the result of a misunderstanding.'

The whole bar had gone silent; locals and visitors alike listened to this larger-than-life figure, speaking slowly and deliberately and with total confidence.

'What do you mean?' spat one of the townies, eager to get a fight going.

'Well,' said Tam, 'you see, these friends of mine took you for gentlemen, and you, sirs, took them for a set of fools, and you are both wrong. So let's just forget all about it.'

The man who had asked what he meant scratched his head in puzzlement and a few of his friends muttered among themselves. There were quite a few looks of bemusement and more than one or two snorts of laughter as people realised that he was simply defusing a dangerous situation. At that point the publican, who had often danced to Tam's fiddle and was wary of the damage a large-scale fight would cause and the cost he would have to bear, decided to help things along.

'Well said, Mister Cramb. Now, who needs a drink? It's on the house.'

So peace broke out at the prospect of a free drink and yet another story was going the rounds about Tam Cramb that very night.

Johnny Faa and Lady Hamilton

This story is believed by some to be based on historical fact and is the origin of a whole set of songs, the best known of which is probably 'The Raggle-Taggle Gypsies'. The earl of Haddington had only one daughter, a braw bonnie lass called Lady Jean

Hamilton, and he doted on her. She grew into her teens as a striking beauty and it was approaching the time when her father thought she should be married. Now, there were a great many titled men who would have been delighted to take her hand in marriage; she was beautiful, rich and well-connected. But her father had resolved to find the best match possible for his bonnie Jean. His choice fell upon Lord Cassilis, a man of considerable standing in Scotland. He was also rich and owned a great deal of land, but Jean herself thought he was far too old for her. She tried to convince her father that she would be much happier with someone nearer to her own age.

'Do ye hae someone in mind?' her father asked when she broached the subject.

'Well, no,' she was forced to reply.

'In that case, I can see nae reason why ye should no marry Cassilis. He's a good match for ye,' said her father.

In truth, Jean did not want to marry Cassilis at all, but there was no one else she could think of that she actually liked. She could hardly tell her father that she was sick to her soul at the thought of being married to old Cassilis, or that she wanted someone much younger. So she asked for some time to think.

'Well, I tell ye, lass, ye can have till tomorrow. He's a grand match for ye, Jean, and I've tellt him I'll let him know soon whether ye are tae be married.' There was a finality in his voice that she recognised. If she couldn't come up with another prospective husband it looked as if she would be stuck with Cassilis after all. The unfortunate thing was that, even among the young men who had been courting her, there was no one she had a particular liking for.

Distraught at her situation, Jean decided to go to the local fair to find some distraction. Unknown to her father, she had gone to neighbouring fairs on quite a few occasions, dressed plainly and often alone. She wanted no maids or other servants with her on such outings. So she changed her clothes and sneaked out of the castle, off to the fair. The village was thronged with people and there were numerous booths selling all kinds of trinkets and sweetmeats. In addition, there was a host of entertainers, musicians, tumblers and dancers, all helping to create a colourful and merry scene. After buying herself some ribbons from a stall, Jean stopped to look at a group of local young lasses who were hiring out to work on farms. Inadvertently, she stepped a little too close to the group. A big, florid farmer, smelling somewhat of drink, came right up to her, attracted by her extreme good looks. Without a word, he pinched her cheek to force her to show her teeth, which were white and even. Taken aback and affronted at this familiarity, she was just about to slap the farmer as hard as she could when a strong, brown-skinned hand reached over her shoulder, took the farmer's wrist and pulled him away.

There, standing beside her, was a powerful young man, who said, 'You'll not be wanting her; she's mine. She's a bit of a scold and a slugabed but I've chased her over three shires.'

As he said this the young man looked straight into the farmer's eyes with a smile. It was a smile that clearly suggested that the farmer took himself off, or there would be trouble. With hardly a look at Jean the farmer just grunted, turned on his heel and walked away.

Jean was even more affronted than she had been and turned to have a good look at this presumptuous stranger. She found herself looking at a handsome young man with the air of a gypsy about him – dark curly hair, flashing black eyes and white teeth. In truth, he was very handsome and she noticed he had a fiddle slung over his shoulder. He spoke before she had a chance to.

'I think you should be bit careful, lassie. Men like that are to be avoided.' As he said this he looked into her eyes and smiled.

Despite her intention to give him a severe telling-off right there and then, Jean felt herself smiling. Why was she smiling? She felt confused and the longer the young man looked at her the more confused she felt.

'My name is Gypsy Johnny,' he said. 'I am a fiddler and I work for one of the better known lords.'

'Well,' she managed to say, 'my name is Jean; I am a lady's maid and . . . and I like fiddle music a lot.' As she said this she found herself blushing furiously. What was going on? She felt excited and just a tiny little bit frightened by the handsome stranger at the same time.

'Well then, Jean,' he said, offering his arm, 'shall we stroll the fair together?' For the next hour or so they wandered round the fair together. They bought themselves some sweetmeats and, after eating them, Johnny decided he would have to play her a tune or two. So, below a tree, forty or fifty yards from the fair crowds, he played her a couple of lively jigs. He then played a lovely slow air that so distracted her that, when he finished, he managed to steal a kiss with no resistance. Jean felt happy and all mixed up, aware that she was about to be betrothed but finding this strolling musician very attractive. As he pulled back from the kiss she looked at him and the thought of this handsome, fit, young man as her husband flashed into her mind. What was she thinking of? At that point someone called to him and, when he turned to reply, Jean ran round the tree and off into the crowds.

Turning back to find the lovely young lass gone, Johnny ran into the crowd and started looking for her. His search was in vain for Jean had made good her escape and hurried back to the castle, flushed and perspiring. The rest of the day she was restless and distracted. The following day, her father again broached the subject of her betrothal to Lord Cassilis, and, believing there could be no hope of finding solace in the arms of a gypsy fiddler, she agreed, but with no enthusiasm. Now, this bothered Haddington; he prided himself on being a practical man but he was very fond of his lovely Jean and was trying to do the best for her that he could. Cassilis was one of the greatest men in the kingdom; he was rich and influential and he was sure to take good care of Jean. The gloomy look on Jean's face as she agreed to the betrothal worried him. However, he put it down to nerves; women were known to be easily distracted, he thought, and once she was married Jean would be fine. So the two were betrothed and a date was set for the wedding.

In the weeks leading up to her marriage Lady Jean took to wandering alone in the hills and woods near her father's castle. Her father and her brothers were concerned at her wan appearance and unusually quiet behaviour. So, one evening, her brothers resolved to take her out of herself. They took her to a ball that was being held by a nearby laird in his castle. Reluctantly, Jean agreed to go; in truth she had found little to excite her since that day she had met the gypsy at the fair. On the way, they passed the village where the fair had been held and, as they passed the tree under which the gypsy had played to her, Jean remembered the soft touch of his mouth on hers and blushed furiously. If anything, this just made her even quieter. Her brothers were sure that an evening of dancing would get her out of the mood she was in.

They arrived at the castle and went in. Already the hall was filling up with people and many of the young lasses came over to wish Jean the best for her forthcoming marriage. She just nodded and thanked them, her eyes wandering vaguely around the room. And there he was, looking straight back at her. Her gypsy. The handsome man came straight over to her and her brothers.

'Aha,' said Robert, the elder of the two, 'how fares it with you, Johnny Faa?'

'I am weel indeed, Lord Robert,' he said. And with a flourish to Jean, 'Will ye not introduce me to this bonnie lass?'

So the speechless Jean was introduced to the man she thought of as her gypsy fiddler.

'This is Sir John Faa of Dunbar, Jean,' said Robert. 'Sir John, may I introduce you to my sister, Lady Jean Hamilton.'

Sir John Faa, she thought as he took her hand and bent to kiss it. He was of a suitable station. She realised she had heard of him;

his family had been ennobled a few generations before after service in battle to the king. He might be a lesser laird but he was a laird. Her hopes soared and as they danced several dances that night she became aware he was as smitten with her as she with him. Her brothers noticed that the bright and sparkling lass they knew her to be had returned. However, they thought that her behaviour with Sir John Faa was a bit too obvious. Despite their remonstrations on the way home late that night, Jean resolved to tell her father that she wanted to marry Johnny Faa.

Her father's reaction to this statement was explosive, to say the least. 'Johnny Faa? Johnny Faa? Ye're tellin me ye want to wed that jumped-up gypsy! He's no near good enough for you, my lass; his fowk were nothing but strolling gypsies a couple o generations back. Naw, naw, I have given my word tae Cassilis and ye will be married to him. As arranged.'

The thought of his beautiful and wonderful daughter marrying someone whose pedigree was of such a limited extent was galling to him. He had always wanted her to marry into one of the best families in the land. Cassilis was even more important than himself; he had the king's ear, and Jean would likely end up as lady-in-waiting to the queen! And here the daft lassie was wanting to throw herself away on a jumped-up gypsy with a tiny castle and hardly any land to speak of. Cassilis owned half of Ayrshire and moved in the highest circles in the land. Jean would marry him. He had given Cassilis his word. At the back of his mind a wee thought crept up. At least Sir John Faa was nearer her in age and . . . 'Dammit!' he roared, 'ye're marrying Lord Cassilis and ye'll like it. Enough.' At that, the enraged Haddington stormed out, leaving his beloved daughter in tears.

From that day till the wedding, guards kept a close eye on Jean; she was unable to get any word to Johnny. He heard soon enough that the wedding was to go ahead and his attempts to get in touch with Jean through her father and brothers were abruptly turned down. At the end of the summer Lady Jean Hamilton married

Lord Cassilis. It was a grand affair with the king himself in attendance, but many there noted how pale and quiet the bride was throughout.

As for Cassilis, he found himself greatly disappointed in his new young wife. She had the reputation of being a bright and lively lass but all he could see in her was listlessness. He was not a bad man; he was old and a bit dull, but he tried to cheer up his young wife with balls and games. Nothing seemed to shake her from her lethargy. He thought that once they had children she would perk up, but after the birth of her first, a boy, she changed little, if at all. The next couple of years saw the birth of a daughter and a second son, but though she seemed to care about them, Lady Jean was as listless as ever. She spent hours on her own in her room with a maid, stitching away at a tapestry. The tapestry was to remind her of Johnny Faa, and at the centre of her sewing was the tree below which they had briefly kissed.

As Lady Cassilis of Maybole Castle she was one of the leading ladies of the land but, despite her husband's efforts, she seemed to have little interest in attending the court. She could easily have become a lady-in-waiting to the queen, he told her, but the idea seemed to hold no attraction for her at all. In the first few years of their marriage Cassilis insisted on her accompanying him to court, but her indifference to the life of court society became too much for him to bear and he began travelling alone, leaving her behind at Maybole Castle. Apart from the time spent sewing, her only pleasure in life was her children. But away from them she was a lonely and dispirited figure. After four years of marriage and the birth of her three children, nothing much seemed to have changed for Lady Jean and she became the subject of gossip, not only amongst the lords and ladies but among the common people too. People said there was something wrong when a beautiful and healthy young mother like Lady Jean seemed to be in a perpetual state of sadness. Cassilis going off on his trips without her only led to further speculation, but the truth of the matter was simply that she was miserable. She had met a man with whom she would happily have spent the rest of her life, but had been forced to marry an old man who brought her no pleasure at all.

One day in 1643 a gypsy came to the castle door. He had long, curly dark hair, an earring and a yellow kerchief on his head. On his back he carried a fiddle. He rang the bell at the great door of the castle and a doorman came out to see who was there.

'Good day, sir,' said the gypsy, doffing his hat and making a great show of bowing. 'I'm a strolling minstrel and the rest of my troupe are just over the hill. Lord Cassilis has sent for us to come and play in the castle.'

The doorman was a bit puzzled by the gypsy's appearance. Lord Cassilis was a devout Presbyterian and was known to have little time for fripperies like music.

'Are ye you sure ye hae the right place?' he asked the gypsy. 'His lordship is off at the court in Edinburgh.'

'Oh, aye,' replied the gypsy with a smile, 'Lord Cassilis himself asked us to come here to Maybole Castle. I'll play you a tune.'

At that, he swung his fiddle over his back, took the bow in his left hand and started to play an ancient ballad. It was a ballad he had played at the fair for Jean, five summers before. Up in her own room working on her beloved tapestry, Jean heard the familiar notes. It couldn't be Johnny, she thought, as she ran to the window. Looking down, she saw the familiar figure playing the violin at the castle gate. The blood rushed to her face and her breath grew short. She ran down through the castle to the gate as the haunting sounds of the old tune rang through the building.

Coming to the entrance of the castle just as the last notes of the old song died away, she barked at the doorman, 'I will handle this myself; leave us.'

There they stood, Jean and Johnny Faa, looking at each other and each of them flushed at the sight of the other.

'I'm here to take you awa, Jean,' he said. 'Just about the whole country o Scotland kens that you're no happy with this man. I have my men in the wood behind the hill. Will ye come? Ye know fine well that I love you, and I am sure that you love me just the same.'

Her heart pounding and her chest tightening, she gasped, 'I'll have to leave my bairns . . .'

'Bring them with ye,' he broke in.

'No, no, that cannae be. Cassilis might just let me go but if we took his bairns we would be hunted down like animals.'

She turned to look back into the castle. She loved her children, but she knew that the only chance of happiness she would ever have in this life was to go with this handsome young man who loved her so much.

'If I'm to come, we must go now – this instant,' she said firmly.

At that, Johnny turned away and gave a shrill whistle. Over the brow of the hill came a mounted man leading a fine gray stallion. Johnny mounted his horse and helped her up in front of him. She almost wept as his arms clasped around her and they turned to ride away. As they came over the top of the hill another five mounted men awaited them. The group set off at a slow pace away from Maybole Castle. One of Johnny's men had been keeping an eye on the castle for months and they were sure that Lord Cassilis would be detained in Edinburgh for a few days more.

They had only been gone an hour or so when Lord Cassilis returned unexpectedly, with a dozen armed men at his back. His business at the court had been postponed and he had headed home. It was only at this stage that the servants in the castle realised that Lady Jean was missing. Cassilis was in a fury. Where had she gone? The doorman told his master that a young long-haired gypsy had come to the castle and that the lady herself had insisted on talking to him. He had seen nothing else of what had happened. The poor man was terrified out of his wits and was lucky that Cassilis did not have him killed there and then. Then a laddie who worked in the kitchen stepped up and said he had seen the lady head off towards Cumnock, sitting on the gypsy's horse with him. Calling for fresh horses and summoning more armed retainers from the castle, Cassilis headed off towards Cumnock with over thirty armed men. Ahead of them, sure there was no chance of pursuit, the two lovers were delighting in each others' company on the back of Johnny Faa's grey stallion, his men riding a little ahead.

They never had a chance. Before they were even aware of what was happening, Lord Cassilis and his men bore down on them at a place still called the Gypsy Slips, less than ten miles from Maybole. The small group was surrounded and captured with hardly a fight, such was the overpowering strength of Cassilis. Johnny Faa and his men had their arms bound and their feet tied under their horses' bellies and were led off back towards Maybole. But not before Cassilis rode up to the younger man and smashed him in the face with his mail-clad glove. As the blood ran down her lover's face, Lady Jean was hoisted up in front of one of Cassilis's men, the entire event taking place in near silence. Cassilis was in a mad rage but had nothing to say to his wife; as for his rival, well, deeds would speak loudest of all . . .

Back to the castle the silent cavalcade rode. Johnny Faa's plan had backfired and he knew fine well what his fate was to be. Never mind that Jean loved him; he had gone off with another man's wife. And that man was one of the greatest barons of Scotland, a man with the power of life and death over all who inhabited his lands. Faa had been caught red-handed. So later that day, there before Maybole Castle, Sir John Faa and his faithful men were hanged from the branches of a single tree as Lady Jean howled at her implacable husband for mercy. There was to be no mercy.

Having taken his revenge on the upstart gypsy laird, Cassilis turned his attention to his faithless wife. Aware that Faa had roused her in ways that were beyond him, he handed down his

39

judgement on his wife. Clad in a simple dress of hodden gray she was to be locked up in a room in the highest tower of Maybole Castle, there to stay with no contact with her children or husband until she died. Cassilis went so far as to call in a mason to carve likenesses of Faa and his men in the walls of that tower room, so Jean would never be able to forget what had happened. And there for many years Lady Jean Cassilis lived alone, weeping gently as she continued to work on the tapestry she had started so many years earlier – the tapestry that spoke of her love for the gypsy fiddler and the love he had for her. The tapestry grew as dark as her thoughts, the dominant colour being that of the red blood Johnny had spilled when Cassilis struck him at the Gypsy Slips. Occasionally, as the years passed, she would hear her children ride out of the castle and though she could catch glimpses of them from the high window of her tower prison, she never talked to them again.

Notable Fiddlers

⟫—◇—⟪

There have been many famous Scottish fiddlers over the past few hundred years but none so weel-kennt as Niel Gow, who features in several stories here. In many ways he exemplifies traditional Scottish culture: straight-spoken, egalitarian and driven by common sense. During Niel Gow's life (1727–1807) Scotland was in the throes of the Enlightenment, the philosophical movement that helped define the modern world and laid the basis for modern economics and sociology. In this period Scottish traditional culture developed along new lines, without losing continuity with the past. In the works of such men as Allan Ramsay, Roberts Fergusson and Burns we can see the development of a magnificent indigenous literature, securely rooted in the majority language of the people – Scots. Burns, though no virtuoso, played the fiddle himself; he clearly had a deep and sympathetic understanding of Scotland's music, which allowed him to create so many timeless songs. No one knows how many actual tunes he 'improved' but it is clear that he was no mean musician. There are other notable figures from the period like Pate Bailie, whose career was, to put it mildly, a bit up and down; given what we know of his character, this is not surprising. The popularity of dancing and the need for music to accompany gave many fiddlers a living.

Niel Gow was followed by his son Nathaniel and others, such as Samson Duncan and Duncan McKercher, known as the Atholl Paganini. Others in the same period who stood out are Peter Milne and William Thomson, and people still remembered earlier fiddlers like Johnstone of Turnmuir. Later in the nine-teenth century we have Scott Skinner, whose career took him overseas, where his playing was highly popular amongst the Scots diaspora. He also, like many other noted fiddlers, played a wide variety of music and performed in music halls as well as at dances, balls and concerts. Less famous musicians such as Tam Cramb and Dancey MacKenzie seem to have been every bit as colourful as their more famous brother fiddlers.

Niel Gow's Rustic Wit

The most famous of all the Scottish fiddlers was Niel Gow, from Inver, near Dunkeld in Perthshire, one of the most beautiful spots in all of Scotland. He was born in 1727, the son of a handloom weaver, and, despite his father's wish for him to follow the same trade, Niel was irresistibly drawn towards music. From an early age he showed great talent; by the time he was thirteen he had developed considerable skill by listening and observing anyone and everyone in the immediate area who could play the fiddle. His first instrument was a simple kit, or box fiddle, an instrument which in time served as a learning instrument for his own sons, who all became fiddlers, though none with quite the talent of their father. His reputation grew from his early teens, when he won a local fiddling competition, and in time he became feted throughout all of Scotland. He was as welcome in the great houses as he was in any humble cottage.

Stocky, open-faced and powerful, Niel was a friendly and enthusiastic man; the combination of his attractive personality and great talent made him a true living legend in eighteenth-century Scotland. His skill in playing seems to have been in his command of melody and the sheer power of his playing, which he often interjected with a loud 'Hooch', as a sign of enthusiasm and encouragement to the dancers. Although he was, like many another Scot, fond of a drop or more of whisky, he was known to be a social drinker and never fell into the vice of solitary drinking, a fate that has befallen so many other musicians past and present.

During his long life he met many eminent people, not least Scotland's national bard, Rabbie Burns, who came to visit him in 1787 on his tour of Scotland. Gow seemed to have shared Burns' disdain for 'airs and graces', as is shown in one particular story from the 1790s, by which time Niel was approaching sixty years of age. Graham of Orchill, a gentleman by the reckoning of the time, was a more than competent fiddler and would occasionally take great pleasure in visiting Gow in his cottage for a wee 'session'. After one such evening's playing, accompanied no doubt by the odd dram, the talk had turned to the revolution in France, and the fear that the same could happen in Britain. Gow remarked, 'Troth, Orchill, ye play weel – be thankfu, for if the French should overrun our country, you and I can win our bread [by playing music], which is more than mony o the grand folk can say.'

There are many instances of Gow's ready wit in the company of his 'betters', which show him to have been a man who would not play up to the aristocracy. It is perhaps a testament to the fundamentally egalitarian basis of much Scottish culture that so many of his sayings in such situations have survived. However, these incidents do not show him to have been particularly anti-aristocratic, merely someone who had no time for pretension and who took people as he found them.

For much of his life Niel was quite closely involved with the dukes of Atholl and other aristocratic families. His talent and fame made him a celebrity in contemporary Scotland and he was a regular visitor to Blair Drummond Castle, the home of the dukes of Atholl. One time, having been asked by the duchess of Atholl to listen to her daughter Lady Charlotte Drummond playing the piano, the fiddler commented, 'That lassie o yours, me leddie, has a guid ear.' At that point, some gentleman who was there, no doubt looking to ingratiate himself with the duchess, interjected, 'I thought, Niel, you had more manners than to call the duchess's daughter a lassie.'

'Whit would I call her?' came the reply. 'I nivver heard that she was a laddie.'

This no doubt put the man's gas at a wee peep, as the saying has it, but the Drummonds were well used to a lack of formality on Gow's part. The duke, in particular, seems to have treated him as a social equal, in some situations at least.

One time when the duke was showing him a room in Blair Castle that had cost £100 to have lacquered – a fortune at the time – Niel said, 'Ach, I'll show ye a room in my ain hoose that took a lot mair than that tae finish.'

He then took the duke to the kitchen in his cottage by the Tay and showed it to him, saying, 'The finish on this wee room has taken monie hundreds of cartloads o peat tae get tae this state – warth a lot mair than yer hundred pounds.'

This shows his sense of humour, but at other times he was hardly backward in remonstrating with the social crowd that hung around the castle. One evening there was a ball being held, for which, as usual, Niel had been hired to play, along with an accompanist on the 'bass' violin, or cello. Supper was announced but quite a few of the fashionable crowd, particularly the ladies, were reluctant to leave the dancing. Supper was announced a second time and, at that point, Niel, becoming a bit narked, put up his bow and announced to the company, 'Gang doun to yer supper, ye daft limmers, and dinnae hold me reelin here, as if hunger and drouth were unkennt in the land – a body can get naethin done for you.' After a few hours of playing our Niel was in need of food – and a dram or two – to keep himself going, and he had no hesitation at all in letting his audience know all about it.

Although no slave to the demon drink, Niel was fond of a glass or two of whisky as can be seen in his famous tune, 'Farewell to Whisky', which he composed after a government act of 1799 substantially increased the price of malted barley, the main ingredient of malt whisky. The ban was a result of crop failure and was a temporary measure, but it was seen by many as an attempt to stamp out the widespread cottage industry of whisky making. It was thought by the majority of the people who drank it that the end of this peatreek industry would see both a drop in quality and a rise in price. Niel, like most people of his days, preferred the whisky that was made in glens and cottages throughout the land to the industrially-produced spirits the government wanted people to drink, to ensure they could collect their taxes. The following year, however, the crop recovered, the price of malt came down and malt whisky was once again freely available. It seems likely that Niel was having a bit of a joke with the name of the air. However it is extremely doubtful that the making of peatreek, or illicit whisky, stopped even for a year, though it is likely there was a severe shortage. It took a while longer for the government to suppress the peatreek industry; it continued till the 1830s, when several of the more notable 'peatreekers' took out government licenses and began to produce legal whisky. It would appear that the Scotch whisky industry attained its pre-eminent reputation because it was founded by people who had learned their trade in the peatreek bothies.

A story is told of Gow coming home from a big dance at Ruthven when he met with an old friend at the bridge over the river Almond. His friend commented on the length of the road he had before him. Niel, who was a bit fou, as the saying goes, replied, 'Deil may come for the length of the road. It's only the breadth of it that's fashin me now.' Something of the same idea was reported by the English poet Robert Southey about the time the duke of Atholl had just paid for a new road from Dunkeld to Perth. Hearing someone praising the new road, which was much straighter than the old country way with its twists and turns, Niel said, 'They may praise your braid roads that gangs by them. For my part, when I've got a wee drappy at Perth, I'm just as lang getting hame by the new road as the auld ane.' He was jokingly referring to the fact that many a night he had come home zig-zagging back and forward across the road all the way home.

The friend he met at the bridge over the Almond at Ruthven later mentioned their meeting that night, saying, 'I think, Niel, ye were the waur o drink that nicht.'

'Tosh,' replied our hero, 'I may hae been fou but I wasnae the waur o it.'

The taking of strong drink has long been common across all social boundaries in Scotland. One time when the duchess of Gordon complained of feeling a bit giddy and that she had a murmuring her head, Niel replied, 'Faith, I ken something o that myself, your grace. When I've been fou the night afore, ye wad think that a bike o bees was bizzing in my bonnet the next morning.' Niel has maybe been associated a bit too much with drunkenness due to a line in the lyrics of the song written to his tune 'Farewell to Whisky', which says he 'dearly loued the Atholl brose'. Atholl brose is a drink made of whisky, oats and cream. The words were written by a minister's wife in Dundee, who never met Gow, but there is no doubt he definitely was fond of a dram.

Niel Gow's Fiddle

All musicians like to play the best available instrument and Niel Gow was no different. Some time early in the 1780s, during one of his many visits to Edinburgh to play at the great balls there, Niel was invited to a party by the wife of an army colonel. She was well known in society circles and had arranged a soiree for all the finest musicians currently in the capital. Niel and his brother Donald went to the address they had been given, but ended up at the back of the house at the kitchen door. As ever, they were rather plainly dressed and were obviously 'from the country'. They were shown into the kitchen and a servant was sent to the lady of the house to say that a couple of rustic characters had arrived looking for her. Left alone in a small room of the vast kitchen, Niel looked around and noticed an old fiddle hanging on the wall. It was a fine-looking instrument and appeared to be Italian. Intrigued, he took it down from the wall, took out his own bow and struck a couple of notes.

'Heavens, man,' said Donald, 'that's a brilliant sound.'

Niel thought so too and dashed off a snappy reel.

'Heavens, Donald, did ye ever hear a fiddle wi a sound like this. It's absolutely brilliant.' So saying, he began to play his favourite tunes, one after the other. He was so rapt in the sound of this magnificent instrument, and Donald was standing there listening with a silly grin listening to the marvellous music, that they didn't even notice when the servant lass came back into the room to ask them upstairs. He heard not a word, so caught up was he in the music. The gathered party upstairs heard the wonderful music and, one by one, they came downstairs till the kitchen was nearly full. At last the hostess had to ask him to stop, but on he played till the servant lass had to take him by the arm, breaking his rapt concentration.

'Och, ma'am, that is some fiddle; I dinnae think I've ever heard a better one in my life,' said the great fiddler, turning the instrument round and round in his hands.

'Well, fair enough, Mr Gow. But I think it would be better played upstairs in the drawing room. Please bring it with you,' replied the lady.

So the entire party trooped upstairs and the night's entertainment commenced, officially. And what a night! Gow played like a man possessed, inspired by the sound of this magnificent violin. In between tunes he kept looking closely at the instrument, so taken was he with it.

At last the night came to an end and Niel, not for the first time, was the last to leave. He was still going on about the quality of the fiddle when the host said, half-jocularly, 'If you think so highly o that fiddle, Mr Gow, what would you say to swapping it for your own?'

Neil needed no second bidding. In a flash he had his own instrument out of its bag and thrust it into the gentleman's hands. He leaned over and grabbed the other one from the nearby table where it lay and stuck it into his green bag. He hung the bag around his neck and shook the colonel briefly by the hand before disappearing off into the night at a good pace. It had taken less than thirty seconds. The colonel was left standing, speechless. The instrument was later discovered to be a Gasparo da Sola, a fine Italian instrument indeed, made by the great Italian craftsman Gasparo Bertoletti, one of the earliest true geniuses of violin-making. And it suited Niel fine!

We can't be sure exactly how the colonel responded to this exchange at the time, but later it seems he greatly valued the fiddle he had got from the great fiddler. He even took the fiddle on campaign in the Napoleonic Wars and it survived active service in Egypt, Spain and Portugal before being brought back to Scotland. Even in the famous retreat from Corunna under General Sir John Moore, when the troops were ordered to abandon everything but their weapons, the colonel carried the fiddle on his back under his cloak!

Tak Yer Time!

Although he is perhaps the most famous fiddler ever to pick up the bow in Scotland, it was well understood that when it came to reading music Niel was no great shakes. One well-known tale illustrates this quite well. The great man was playing at a ball in Glamis Castle when one of the gentlemen there brought out the sheet music for a set of tunes he had written himself, in honour of the evening's hostess. The set was entitled 'Lady Glamis' Medley'. Obviously, it would be a dreadful gaffe not to play the piece, but Niel was a wily character when he needed to be.

'I dinna know the piece,' he said darkly to the man holding up the sheet music.

'But it's all here,' said the gentleman, a bit confused. He presumed that such a virtuoso of the fiddle as the great Niel Gow must be totally in command of written music. As Niel just stood looking at him, he handed the music to the maestro and went to join the rest of the company on the dance floor.

Niel turned to his second fiddler, a young pupil of his by the name of Cuthbert.

'Och, this is in B flat,' said Niel. 'Ye ken I'm no at ma best in thon key. You start it up while I just replace ma first string. It's kind of gone dead on me.'

So, as the great man restrung his fiddle, the young Cuthbert started off the Strathspey accompanied by the cello player, Marshall. By the time they had played it through twice Niel had caught the tune by ear and he joined in with total command of the melody. The medley then changed to a reel. At which point Niel's first string started bothering him again. He stopped playing and, turning his back on the audience, pretended to tune the recalcitrant string. Just as the first playing of the reel came to an end and started all over again – wonder of wonders – Niel was back in tune and struck up the reel along with Cuthbert. No one in the audience noticed a thing and it was only because Cuthbert eventually told an old friend of what went on that night that the story was ever told.

Something Similar

Niel's sense of humour definitely bordered on the mischievous and, as the previous story shows, he could be a bit fly. He was once in an Edinburgh fiddle shop on the lookout for a new bow. As usual, he was dressed in a plain fashion and looked nothing remarkable. He asked to see some bows and the shopkeeper presented him with a selection. He selected one, and asked if he could have a violin and a piece of music to try it out.

The shopkeeper obliged and handed them over. The music was none other than Niel's latest composition 'Pease and Beans', a complicated and difficult piece.

'I'll tell you what, my man,' he said, smiling, 'that piece of music there is the very latest piece by the great fiddle player, Niel Gow.' Pausing to let this sink in, and aware that this was a hard piece to play, the shopkeeper decided to have a bit of fun with this teuchter, a term used in Scots to describe a simple country-man. He went on, smiling, 'If you can play that by sight without any mistakes, I'll give you the bow for free.'

The look on his face showed what he thought the chances of that happening were!

'Och, well,' said Niel, 'I dinnae mind trying to have a go at that.'

So the music was put on a stand and Niel tucked his bow under his chin, lifted his bow arm, then dropped it again to peer closely at the sheet of music. Behind his back the shopkeeper sneered.

Then, with a flourish, Niel went into the tune – straight off, without the semblance of a hesitation, not once but twice.

'But, that's marvellous,' stuttered the shopkeeper. 'Your sight reading is right remarkable.'

'Weel, maybe,' replied Neil with a grin, 'though I kind of got used tae the notes while makin it up.'

'You – you're Niel Gow?' the shopkeeper gasped. 'The great Niel Gow, here in my wee shop. Oh, let me shake you by the hand, sir. You are welcome indeed to that bow and long use may you have of it. Niel Gow in my wee shop,' he repeated, clutching his visitor's hand and looking at him with admiration.

The upshot was that Neil got his bow and the shopkeeper got a lot of custom when the story went the rounds. But his greatest pleasure was in knowing he had shaken the hand of the great man himself.

A Fiddlers' Stramash

One time Niel had been playing at Morton Hall near Edinburgh and was walking back to the city with his fiddle hanging round his neck in its customary green bag. It had been a long night's playing and he was passing Powburn just as dawn was breaking when he met up with a scruffily-clad man.

'Ye're early abroad,' said the stranger, fixing his gaze on the bag round Niel's neck.

Niel, as ever, was happy to talk to strangers and replied, 'Well, it's more like I'm late. I have just come from a ball at Morton Hall, where I've been fiddlin aw nicht.'

The stranger looked hard at him and said, 'Would you have onie snuff aboot ye?'

'Och, aye,' said Niel with a smile, and stuck both his hands in his jacket pockets to find his snuff box. Seeing his chance, the stranger grabbed at the bag round Niel's neck. With one tug the drawstring broke and the man turned on his heels and ran off. Niel gave no thought to the fact that the man was about half his age; he chased after him. Given his habit of walking everywhere, Gow was still a fit and healthy man and, though the other man outstripped him over the first few hundred yards, it was soon apparent Niel would catch him up. The thief kept looking over his shoulder at the pursuing fiddler. Niel's heart was in his mouth. What if this thief decided just to throw his fiddle away – it could be damaged. They kept on running but the man in the lead was getting winded. It was only a matter of time before the powerful Gow caught up with his attacker. He grabbed the man round the neck from behind, nearly throttling him. Still the stranger hung on to the precious violin.

'Let me go; ye're near stranglin me,' cried the stranger, panting with exhaustion. Gow released his grip and the man fell to his knees, sucking in great breaths of air but still holding on to the instrument. 'Honest, I'm no a thief. I'm a fiddler, like yersel, an I just gave in tae temptation.'

'Whit d'ye mean, temptation? Do ye no hae a fiddle o yer ain?' growled Niel, standing close over the man. 'You could gang to prison for a trick like this. Gie me ma fiddle.'

Reluctantly, the man handed the fiddle over and looked up at Gow with sadness written all over his face.

'I was jist really borrowin the fiddle, ye ken,' he muttered, a catch in his voice.

'Borrowin, borrowin,' roared Niel, 'ye blackguard, ye stole ma fiddle fae roun ma ain neck. It's the jile for you, ma mannie.'

'Oh please no, no that. A've been there afore – no for stealin, mind, an I widnae want to go back there ever, please mister,' he pleaded. 'I'm at the end o ma tether. I've had tae pawn ma ain fiddle an nane o ma friends can help me. I just thought that if I had a fiddle again I could earn some money tae feed ma wife an bairns. It's drivin me daft; they're goin hungry, an I just thought I could mak some money tae feed them.'

'What, ye've nae friends that can help you?' demanded Niel. 'Could you not get the loan of a fiddle, mannie?'

'Ach, they aw ken fine that I'm mair trouble than I'm worth. Ma mither aye said I'd end up on the end o a rope,' the man replied mournfully.

Niel was looking down at this miserable creature at his feet and his kind heart was touched despite his considerable anger at the attempted theft. 'Well, I'll no try and send ye there, even if you deserve it.' He stuck his hand in his pocket and pulled out a handful of silver.

Handing it to the distraught creature still kneeling in the road, he said, 'Here, tak this, but for Heaven's sake never try and steal anither man's fiddle. It's as bad as tryin to steal his child.'

The kneeling man took Niel's hand in both his own and, as he bent his head, a tear splashed onto the back of Niel's hand. Ever a sympathetic and kindly man, despite what had gone before, Niel was touched.

'Ach, wheesht, wheesht, mannie, dinnae bather yerself. Look, just tell me whaur ye live an I'll see if I can give ye a bit help.'

'Thank you, thank you,' the man burst out, 'ye're awfy kind. I live up the Morocco Close in the Cowgate, one up. You know,' he said, getting to his feet, 'I used to play in the theatre over at the Shakespeare Square. I'm no a bad fiddler, really.'

Intrigued at this, Niel asked. 'What can ye play?'

'Och, aw sorts,' replied the stranger. 'I can read anything put in front o me and can pick up a new tune as quick as ye like.'

'Oh, aye,' said Niel, thinking the man seemed confident enough, and wondered if he might be a reasonable player after all, 'and what's your name?'

'My name is Pate Baillie,' replied the other, 'and if ye ask anybody about the town, they'll tell you I can play the fiddle.'

The two carried on into town together and, before parting, Gow promised he would call round to Baillie's home later that day. He was as good as his word and arrived carrying his beloved Gasparo violin. As soon as he heard Baillie play, he realised that he was a fine musician indeed. Despite how they met, he resolved to help the Edinburgh man and within days had managed to get Pate's fiddle out of pawn for him and set him up with a long-term gig in the Theatre Royal orchestra. From then on, whenever anyone mentioned Niel Gow, Pate Baillie would declare that he wasn't just the best Scottish fiddler, he was the finest man in all the land.

At the time of this episode, in the early 1790s, Niel Gow was nearly seventy years old and Pate not even half that age!

Pate Baillie

Edinburgh was a great place for fiddlers through the seventeenth and eighteenth centuries. If you wanted to make a real success you came to Edinburgh to play at the numerous balls, and it was here that a great many collections of fiddle tunes were published. Here too was the greatest selection of shops where both instruments and music could be found for sale. The popularity of dancing, and hence fiddle music, had spread through all levels of society and, though no longer the capital of an independent nation, Edinburgh continued as the social, political and financial centre of Scotland. Musicians, good ones anyway, could make a better living here than anywhere else in Scotland. However, the countryside around Edinburgh was, like much of the rest of Scotland, a hotbed of fiddling too, and one of the best-known Scottish fiddlers came from Loanhead, a few miles to the south of the capital. This was the famous, or notorious, Pate Baillie, who was born in 1774 and became known as the 'the Fiddling Tinker'. In fact, he was apprenticed as a stone mason and worked for an uncle for some years, during which time he helped to build Edinburgh University's Old Quad, still standing on South Bridge. Pate, though, was not a man for regular hours and wanted a freer lifestyle. However, he never was a tinker – a term initially used for travelling tinsmiths and later given to all the travelling people of Scotland. Pate was neither a traveller nor a tinsmith. The trade he took up, apart from fiddling, was that of a horner – a maker of the traditional horn spoons that were long favoured by the people of Scotland before the rise of industrialism, when metal cutlery became affordable for the majority.

However, it was as a fiddler that Pate gained his reputation – a job that (like that of horner) was self-employed and made him his own master – a fact that allowed him the freedom to enjoy other aspects of life for which he had a liking, such as fishing on the North Esk and taking the odd dram. He liked more than one at a time, and nothing unusual about that. In fact, it was said of Pate that he could play the fiddle as well on his back as he could standing up, which says a great deal for his musical technique, if nothing else! He was also known to have a short temper and on more than one occasion fell out with fellow fiddlers.

Something else he was known for was being able to improvise at the drop of a hat. This was known as extemporising variations, and one story shows just how talented Pate was in this respect. He was playing on the ferry between Leith and Burntisland in Fife when a gentleman asked him to play a certain tune. This he did with vigour; then the gentleman promised him a considerable amount of money if he could play ten variations on the piece. Pate needed no second bidding and, when he had dashed off twenty variations with no hesitation, the gentleman held up his hands for the fiddler to stop playing. 'Enough, enough,' he laughed, 'you have done very well indeed and here's twice what you were promised. Much more of this and you would empty my pockets.'

Pate became very well known at balls, barn dances, fairs and weddings in the Lothians. Like so many other Scottish fiddlers, he was as happy to play for the gentry at a ball in a big house as he was to play for farm-workers at a barn-dance or harvest-home. One time he had been contracted to play in a Berwickshire town he had never visited before and, being a convivial sort, he got in company once the gig was over. He found himself in a barn the following day – potless – he'd spent all his wages, and, looking into the local howff (pub), he saw there was nobody that had been there the night before – even the landlord was away up to Edinburgh on business and the lass behind the bar did not know him. He was wandering along in the evening, thinking he had a long road to walk back to Loanhead, when he heard music – fiddle music. Near the town centre there was a hall he hadn't noticed the day before, all lit up and with the sounds of a band playing for a dance. As an experienced musician he had no trouble getting past the door; he simply showed his fiddle and told the doorman he had come to join in with the band. With his fiddle half hidden under his coat he sidled up to where the band were playing on a small stage. Competition between musicians being what it was, he couldn't be sure of a friendly welcome. The band leader, a man considerably younger than Pate at the time, saw him approach and thought he was just another wandering fiddler, of whom there were many. Truth be told, Pate was not looking his best after the previous night's drinking and a sleep in the hay.

At the next break in the music the band leader decided to have a bit of fun and, turning to wink at the rest of the band, he asked Pate, 'Have you come far, auld man?'

'Och, just a bit,' replied Pate.

'And were there coppers a plenty on your road then?' came the next question.

'Middlin, just middlin,' said Pate, catching on and playing along.

'Well, will you not favour us with a tune then, old fella?' said the band leader, turning to give a big grin to his pals.

'Och, I might dae waur than just try it,' said Pate; and up with the fiddle and on with the bow and into a well-known tune. The band, recognising the tune, came in behind him and the dancers piled onto the floor. Soon the whole hall was full of dancers and everybody was on their feet. The tone and vigour of the fiddler got them all going. At the end of the dance they clapped and cheered and the band-leader put out his hand saying, 'Well, one of two conclusions is certain: ye must be eethir the deil or Pate Baillie.' Needless to say, things went well for the rest of the night and Pate managed to get his coach fare home, and no doubt another glass or two of the cratur, just to keep him going.

Pate was a bit of a showman and, apart from playing flat on his back, which was not always his intent but sometimes just making the best of a bad job, to entertain the audience he would sometimes play the fiddle behind his back, and over his head – the Jimi Hendrix of his day.

Pate was a notable player and a well-known man in and around the capital city, a celebrity in his time; he was extremely upset to read the report of his own death in the paper one day. His good wife Janet consoled him and said, 'Never mind, these things happen.' But, just as luck would have it, a year or two later the same thing happened again and he said, with a tear in his eye, 'Jennet, they hae me deid again.'

At last, though, Pate's time was nearly up. He was almost seventy years old and his health was failing fast. His old friend and fellow-fiddler Geordie Wilson came to see him. They talked about dances they had played at, lasses they had wooed when they were young and all the other reminiscences that make old men happy. Given their line of work, they had much to reminisce about and, despite his ill-health and knowing he was not long for this world, Pate managed to cheer up a bit in Geordie's company. They talked of other musicians, patrons who had paid well (and some who hadn't) and the hours passed pleasantly enough.

At last they began to talk about the tunes they had particularly liked, or that had been particular favourites with audiences. Geordie took out his fiddle and played a few of the tunes they had played over the years.

'It's funny how a sang'll play weel in one place an no another,' commented Geordie.

'Ach, weel,' said Pate, 'I mind my granny used to tell me when I was wee that fowk might seem tae be the same but that we are aw different.'

'Aye, right enough, I suppose,' replied Geordie, 'an I've heard it said often enough ye never can tell.'

They both smiled at this; then Geordie mentioned an old tune that he had only ever played a few times, but that he had always liked.

'Och, I mind that ane fine,' said Pate, on his bed. 'My auld uncle that taught me the fiddle taught me that ane; I used to play it a lot when I was startin oot but I havnae heard it in a lang time now.'

'Weel, there's nae time like the present,' said Geordie, lifting his fiddle and starting in to the tune. Pate's eyes glowed with pleasure and his face was wreathed in a great smile.

'Man,' he said, 'my auld uncle would surely swear at me if I didnae stamp thon tune out richt, but bring the devil himsel here nou an let's see who can stamp it out best!'

So saying, he sat up and reached under his bed to pull out his fiddle. He sat up on the edge of the bed and the two old fiddlers swung into the tune, stamping it out with gusto as they played. Within a couple of days the great Pate Baillie was dead, but right to the last he took great pleasure in his fiddle. There were those who said that he must have gone straight to hell after the life he had led, but that the devil and his demons would have rare music to dance to, with Pate Baillie in their midst.

Pate Baillie and William Thomson

Now, Pate was a man who had a pretty good opinion of himself and this probably increased when he had a collection of his own tunes published in Edinburgh in 1825. He was well known for putting down fiddlers less talented than himself and, as far as he was concerned, that seemed to be anyone not called Peter Baillie! This, combined with his love for a dram, got the better of him on a couple of occasions. One time he was playing with his own band at a ball in Auchendinny, just a few miles southwest of Loanhead. Another band, led by a talented local amateur fiddler by the name of William Thomson, whose speciality was playing strathspeys, was also there. As we will see, Pate didn't always get things his own way.

William Thomson was born at Boghead in Lasswade parish in 1785. Unlike many another notable fiddler of the time, he didn't take up playing the instrument till he was in his teens. He had already left school and started working in the paper mill at Auchendinny when he decided to take up the fiddle. From the very beginning he showed considerable musical ability and pretty soon he got himself a reputation as a fine fiddler. At this time, of course, this meant one thing above all – he was in demand for playing at dances and balls. However, he was unusual in that, although he had what we still refer to as a good ear, he had learned to read new pieces of music on sight, a not-so-common skill in his day, or even now. The fact that he had been steeped in his native music tradition made it a simple thing for one so gifted to catch the natural rhythms of reels, strathspeys and so on. So he was soon getting enough work to be able to live off his music.

Before he got to that stage in his career he had a run-in with Pate Baillie. Now, as we have seen, Baillie was a forceful character indeed and he often took great delight in 'extinguishing' fiddlers whom he considered to be less talented than himself.

He had heard of the new young fiddler from Lasswade, and when he heard that the young lad, still an amateur at the time, was to be playing at the same Auchendinny ball as he was, he no doubt thought that he would be able to put this young whipper-snapper in his rightful place. Now, competition amongst musicians was nothing new then, nor is it unknown now, and they would often vie with each other to show off who was the more able. In those days most people played off sheet music, though in many cases, again like today, it would often be little more than a wee help to the memory in playing familiar tunes. The more unscrupulous fiddlers, of whom our Pate was surely one, would go out of their way to always have a new composition or two written out, which they would use to face down other players. In fact, Pate was quite adept at this and would often have as many as half a dozen unfamiliar tunes written out for just such an occasion. Usually, one or two would suffice for him to 'show up' the competition. Such was his reputation as both a fiddler and a wild man that few tried to get their own back by the same method. As he would always assume the role of leader in any group he joined, it was difficult to stop him taking over and doing his own thing.

The night he came to Auchendinny, however, Pate met his match. He arrived to find the ball there in full swing, with a packed hall dancing blithely away to the very fine music coming from the band: two fiddlers and a cello player up on the stage at the end of the hall opposite the door. Awaiting a break in the music, Baillie made his way over to stand before the stage.

'Good evenin,' he said, looking straight at Thomson.

'Good evening, sir,' said the young fiddler, showing respect for this older figure standing there with his fiddle and what was clearly a portfolio of music.

'Do you know who I am?' demanded Baillie.

In truth, Thomson had an idea who he might be; he had heard enough descriptions of the older fiddler, but he hadn't actually seen him before.

'No, I am sorry, sir, but I dinnae think we have ever met,' he replied with a smile. Baillie's eyes narrowed.

'Hmm, well, I am Pate Baillie and I was wonderin if I micht hae a tune or two with you,' he said.

'It would be an honour, Mr Baillie,' replied Thomson with a bow.

'Right then,' said Baillie, climbing onto the stage, already with a suspicion this laddie was in need of being put in his place. 'We'll jist have a go at a couple of these wee tunes of mine. Ye are a reader I suppose?' he asked, knowing fine well that Thomson was known for this skill.

'Aye, that's fine by me,' said Thomson; Baillie handed him a piece of music to put on his stand, the other fiddler leaving the stage to make way for the 'great man'.

Thomson, aware of what was probably going to happen next, announced to the dancers that they were about to have the pleasure of the great Pate Baillie leading them off in a new tune of his own composition. Celebrity is nothing new and the news was greeted with great enthusiasm by the assembled crowd. One or two of the more seasoned dancers, and the accompanying musicians, knew what Pate was up to. They just smiled.

With hardly a second's hesitation, Baillie launched into the reel he had just handed Thomson. He, of course, knew it off by heart.

To his utter astonishment, he found the younger musician playing along with him as if he been playing the piece for months! He looked at the lad and, sure enough, he was reading the music straight off the page with no hesitation at all. This fired Pate's temper a bit and the fire in the music was caught by the audience. The room began to resound to loud hoochs and cries. Jazz and rock musicians were certainly not the first to be involved in 'cutting' sessions, trying to outdo each other in front of their audiences. At the end of the piece Thomson handed the music to Baillie, thanking him for his contribution.

But Pate wasn't done yet. No, no, not by a long chalk. He felt as if this young man had humiliated him, conveniently forgetting that this was the fate he had intended for the young man himself.

'Och, hoots, laddie,' said Pate, with a big smile, but seething inside, 'ye're such a grand reader let's try another one.' Saying this he handed over another one of his own compositions.

The result was exactly the same. As soon as he struck up, the young fiddler was playing along in perfect pitch and with perfect timing. This was unheard-of. Outwardly grinning, Pate announced to the audience before the next tune that they had a 'braw young fiddler' amongst them. Again he handed over music, trying to catch the young man out. Again Thomson rose to the challenge. The competition between them was now quite obvious; but the resultant playing was fiery indeed and the enthusiasm of the dancers simply grew and grew. At the back of the hall near the door, surreptitious bets were being placed on how soon Pate would overpower the young lad. People from the immediate area were happy to accept such bets.

Again the tune finished to rapturous applause and again Baillie reached into his portfolio. Now though, before starting, he took off his cravat. Things went as before. After that tune, off came his jacket. After the next tune, played in exemplary fashion by both men, Pate rolled up his sleeves. Young Thomson, however, was the picture of calm.

By now the old fiddler was in a furious rage and, in a difficult bit in the next piece, which truth to tell he had only finished composing a few days before, he hit a wrong note. This was followed by another and, desperately trying to regain the melody that Thomson had never wavered from, he hit a third clinker. Some among the crowd cheered!

This was too much. Throwing his bow to one side in a fit of gargantuan rage, Baillie dropped his fiddle on the stage and jumped up in the air. Down he came with both feet on the delicate instrument. Thomson, remembering his duty to the dancers, kept playing the tune till the beetroot-faced Baillie grabbed the music from under his nose and leapt from the stage. Thomson was not finished yet though. Having been through the tune once, he had it and carried on playing till the end of the dance set. He finished to thunderous applause from the hall. Of Baillie there was no sign.

This 'fiddlers' fecht', of course, did no harm to young William's reputation and he and his band were soon booked up for the rest of that season. Never again did Pate Baillie try and cross swords with William Thomson. William went on to have a long and successful career, touring all over Scotland for several years with a dancing master by the name of McGregor, who had actually been born in France. When Thomson eventually died in 1840 he was a well-respected member of his community, a famous fiddler. The great crowd of mourners who came to his funeral at Penicuik showed just how much the people of the area had taken him to their hearts.

A Forfar Fiddler

James Allan was born in 1800 in Forfar. His father made his living as a barber, but James was sent to learn to be a weaver. Weaving was a widespread trade at the time and the folksong 'The Wark o The Weavers' comes from Forfar, which was traditionally a weaving centre. The song's claim that as long as there is a need for clothes there will be a need for weavers has sadly proved untrue. It was in James's life that the hand-loom weavers, who worked in their own cottages and were essentially self-employed, were superseded by factories, where cloth could be manufactured much more cheaply. Luckily for James, his father had been a fair amateur fiddler and had taught his son the rudiments of the instrument at an early age. James soon found himself outstripping his father as a fiddler and was passed on to his cousin Archie, who took him under his wing after James's father died in 1811. Archie's instruction must have been pretty good, for soon James was getting plenty work all over Angus.

Like Niel Gow before him, he was popular with all classes and regularly played at Cortachy Castle, the home of the earls of Airlie, as well as at barn dances, weddings and balls. At forty he married a widow who owned a wee inn at the East Port in Forfar. This could have been a dangerous step for a man who liked a dram but James was basically a canny sort. He was a first-class player and won lots of competitions, but he was extremely intolerant of bad fiddlers. One time he was in company with a bunch of fiddlers having a dram and a bit of a session in his wife's howff. One particular player, a carpenter, kept asking him, 'Do you think my playin is getting better, James? I'm puttin in lots o hours o practise.'

After the third time he asked, James's reply was succinct: 'Damned a bit better an never will be. Stick to the woodwork.'

James eventually became so well known that in 1856 a promoter called Julian Adams teamed him up on a tour with Duncan McKercher, known as the Atholl Paganini. The concert party toured much of the British Isles and were a great hit. The following year James was due to meet Adams after a gig in Inverness. However, as was often the case, then as now, after the gig the band needed to unwind and went off to a friend's house. There, following the old adage of when in Rome do as the

Romans do, they followed local custom and a great deal of whisky was drunk. The band all drank till they fell asleep and the meeting was missed. So, no big tour that year. However, the following year our intrepid Forfar band were in the concert party again and all was going well as they toured England playing in concert halls. That is, it went well until they came to Leamington, when the whole tour fell apart and they had to send for money to get home. Whether this was due to Adams or the band themselves is unclear.

In later years the truth about the disaster at Leamington perhaps came out when James was asked his opinion of the playing of Duncan McKercher. 'Weel,' says James, 'he's a fine player, a capital player, but I cannae be doin wi his Highland diddrie – that wheetie-whittie style o his, ower mony notes for my liking. It's too much like he was trying to imitate the bagpipes.'

In his seventies Jamie became quite ill and was forced to take to his bed. A benefit was held in Dundee's Kinnaird Hall and the reasonable sum of £70 was raised to help the old fiddler. A few weeks later an ex-pupil of his, Dr Moncur, called for a visit.

'How are you doing, Diamond,' asked James, using the nickname he had given Moncur when he was still just a lad.

'Och, I'm fine. James, are ye getting a drink at all these days?' asked the doctor.

'O, michty little,' replied James sadly.

'Well, I have the bottle; would you have the glasses?' asked Moncur with a smile.

'Och, that I do and I must say you're the best man has entered the hoose since I had to lie down.' A convivial night was passed and, for the rest of the four years that James Allan lived, the regular visits of Dr Moncur helped to keep him smiling. The doctor's prescription of plenty good fiddling and a wee drop of whisky were just the thing for the Forfar Fiddler.

Duncan McKercher, the Atholl Paganini

It is often said that Duncan McKercher was born in the same place as Niel Gow – Inver, near Dunkeld in Perthshire. In fact, he was born in the picturesque village of Kenmore, at the east end of Loch Tay, though he did live in Inver for a while. What is certain is that, like Niel Gow before him, he had a great reputation as a fiddler in his own lifetime, and there were even some who thought him to be a better player than his illustrious predecessor. McKercher liked to make a great deal of the fact that he had been taught to play by the great Gow, but there has been some doubt cast on this, as Gow isn't known to have done much teaching towards the end of his life. McKercher was eleven years old when Gow died, so it is possible they knew each other, but there is no doubt that claiming to have been taught by the man considered to have been the greatest of all Scottish fiddlers could have done him no harm at all. McKercher seems certainly to have been a showman par excellence, and what we know about him suggests that he was far ahead of his time in understanding the value of publicity. It might even be fair to say he never allowed the facts to get in the way of a good story.

He was not a man known for playing slow airs; he had a vigorous, fiery style, well suited to the dance music of his time. His spirited approach was probably what led the well-known politician Fox Maule, Baron Panmure, to call him the Atholl Paganini. Maule was a member of the aristocracy, who entered parliament and rose to the position of Secretary of War during the Crimean War, his reputation suffering as a result. Nicknamed 'the Bison' because of his brawny physique and bullish temperament, Maule was a forceful administrator but was often criticised for his insensitivity, especially when he tried to secure favours for a relative who was serving in the Crimea. In later years he became the earl of Dalhousie. Maule had a long lease on Birnam Lodge, a few miles from Dunkeld, and often visited there. He must have heard Duncan at local balls in the big houses of Perthshire, and it is quite possible that he himself hired the fiddler to entertain at Birnam Lodge. Maule was a Freemason, something that McKercher himself was proud to proclaim.

Although McKercher was clearly liked by Fox Maule, there was disagreement about his playing amongst some of his fellow fiddlers. It has been suggested that Maule was moved to the description more by Duncan's showmanship than any resemblance to the playing of the great Italian maestro. James Allan, the Forfar fiddler, played alongside Duncan on tour and he had no good opinion of the other man's bowing style, which he considered too constrained. There were others, though, who thought he played more like Niel Gow than anybody else; this was praise indeed. He couldn't have been that bad: he was the winner of a fiddle competition in 1851, the prize for which was Niel Gow's fiddle. This fiddle still exists and is currently the property of the Gaelic Society of Perth. What is without doubt is that his playing was just the style that was needed for dancing and no doubt this formed the basis of his popularity. Like many another fiddler, though, he couldn't rely totally on his fiddle-playing for a living, and in the 1840s he was employed by the Atholl Estates as what we would now call a tourist guide. Apart from his work in showing throngs of visitors round the gardens of Atholl House, he was still busy playing in the evenings. Living in Dunkeld, he was handy for a lot of work throughout Perthshire and included more than a few concerts in his activities.

Now, we know that Duncan was a man who thought highly of himself and was quite the showman. He always took great pleasure in playing the well-known tune 'The Mason's Apron'; it gave him the opportunity to put on a bit of a show. He would pause to actually put on his own mason's apron (part of the Freemasons' costume) before playing the tune. Though quite small in stature, Duncan was always well turned-out and he would stand before the audience in a long black coat, with a tartan sash over his right shoulder and the apron round his waist, extending the moment before he launched into the lively tune. This became a great favourite with audiences throughout Scotland; on some occasions he would be in full Highland dress with the masons' apron as well. In fact this became his show-stopper and, at the end, he would throw his arms over his head, holding high the fiddle in his left hand and the bow in his right. He was clearly proud to be known as a mason, and, while their secretive ways in more recent times have caused many people to have misgivings about their activities, they were undoubtedly a radical organisation in the closing years of the eighteenth century. Much has been written about masonic influence on the French Revolution, for instance, and Rabbie Burns, an undoubted radical of his time, was also a mason. So even if these days some people see them as a self-serving mutual support scheme for their members, it would seem things were different in Duncan's time: despite his widespread fame and popularity in his fiddle-playing days, he ended up in a poor house in Colinton, Edinburgh. The popularity of his rendition of 'The Mason's Apron' also suggests that many of his audience might have been members of the numerous masonic lodges of the mid-nineteenth century, which seem to have been less elitist than today.

Now Duncan, as well as being on the small side, had rather weak eyesight. But, being vain, he was not inclined to wear spectacles except when absolutely necessary. He could see well enough to read music when he had to, but in dim light his eyesight could lead him into some odd situations. Like many another musician he enjoyed the occasional glass or two of spirits. One time he had been playing at a dance in Blairgowrie, a few miles from Dunkeld, and afterwards went off with some friends and fellow musicians to the Queen's Hotel.

That night the drink of choice was hot toddy, a concoction of whisky, hot water and sugar or honey. Although nowadays con-sidered primarily a medicinal drink for the relief of colds and flu, toddies were for a long time very popular in Scotland, particularly in the winter time, when their consumption could be suggested as a preventative. After a few drinks the entire company moved to the billiard room, which was rather dim. In those days the accepted way of sweetening the drink was to put a cube of sugar in it. Duncan inadvertently picked up a billiard chalk and, to his friends' delight, dropped it into his glass. He had a great deal of trouble trying to figure out just why his toddy was so cloudy and tasted so bland. The fact that he finished it was probably down to the toddies he had already consumed; but his friends at least stopped him sucking on the billiard chalk!

Although he seems to have been a sometimes difficult character, there is little doubt he was popular in Perthshire. In the early 1860s he had the great pleasure of obtaining the lease of Niel Gow's old cottage at Inver from the then duke of Atholl. This was seen as a definite mark of respect from Perthshire's leading family and must have made him a happy man indeed. He lived there until his death in 1873. In the intervening years he continued playing and teaching and he also published three collections of his own compositions, some of which are thought by scholars to have been 'lifted' from other players. To the last, Duncan seems to have been a bit of a lad.

And Another Perthshire Fiddler

Throughout the eighteenth and nineteenth centuries fiddle-playing was popular all over Scotland. Every area had its favourites, but Perthshire does seem to have produced quite a few whose fame has lasted. One of these was Samson Duncan, born in 1767, the son of the miller at Kinclaven and one of seven children. John Duncan, his father, had a few acres of land, so, although he had seven children, not a particularly large family for the time, they were not forced to live in the poverty that certainly afflicted many at the time. John Duncan was very fond of music, though he himself had never learned to play an instrument. From an early age Samson showed signs of musical ability and the story is told that his very first instrument was one he made himself out of an old piece of board, over which he stretched lengths of horsehair. Somehow or another he managed to tease some tunes from this unlikely instrument; when one of his older brothers brought a real fiddle to the house the tiny Samson, whose hands could hardly reach the length of the finger board, managed to play recognisable tunes on it. This astounded his father and the rest of the family, who had till then thought of his 'board' as being merely a child's plaything. Here they were finding out that the wee laddie had music in his fingers and lugs (ears) as well as in his blood.

There was only one thing to do – the lad had to have a teacher. His first steps in learning to play the instrument properly came at the hands of a local man, who at least taught him a scale or two. His next tutor was a local cooper by the name of Saunders Borlum. It seems that whatever the cooper taught the lad was absorbed at their first contact. Samson's innate grasp of music made reading on sight a simple matter for him; it was commented on by one of Borlum's acquaintances, after watching Samson read a new piece of music straight off. The friend told Borlum, 'Saunders, ye're cuttin yer ain girths there.' By this he meant that Borlum was spiting himself by encouraging a learner who clearly had the potential to be a much better player than himself, and would therefore soon be capable of picking up gigs that might have gone originally to the cooper himself. Samson's keenness to learn can be judged by the fact that Borlum lived ten miles from Kinclaven; the youngster had a twenty-mile walk every time he went for a lesson. In those far-off times money was a relatively scarce commodity, self-sufficiency in growing food was the norm, and John Duncan paid for his son's lessons in oatmeal. This seems a smart idea for a miller!

By now, it was becoming obvious to all who knew him that Samson had the makings of a fine fiddler. So he was soon following a well-worn path. Dancing was hugely popular with all levels of Scottish society and even some of the stricter Presbyterian sects would allow a little of it at weddings, though generally with the sexes dancing separately. It is probably from this time that an old joke first arose. A strict Presbyterian minister rose in the pulpit one Sunday. 'We are all sinners,' he roared at the top of his voice. 'It has come to my attention that some of ye have strayed gey far from the path of righteousness. I have been told that some of you have been making love standing up. This cannot be tolerated as it might lead you into the foul sin of dancing! It must stop!'

However, the rest of the population flocked to balls and dances, ceilidhs and barn-dances. Dancing was the most popular form of entertainment in Scotland and musicians were in great demand all over. Perthshire was the same as everywhere else and soon young Samson was being hired to play at weddings. The music for these weddings stayed pretty much the same. Reels and jigs, strathspeys and schottisches were all popular, the music itself all being essentially Scottish. The same repertoire was used for the barn-dances and, though the big balls held by the gentry and the aristocracy might have one or two more fancy dances thrown in, essentially they followed the same pattern. Because of his good sight reading and fast ear Samson was popular with other musicians, as well as finding a ready and appreciative audience for his playing. Soon he was getting plenty of work and began saving to take his next step. Soon after his seventeenth birthday he had saved up three pounds and put his plan into action. This was a considerable amount of money at the time, the average weekly wage for a labourer being just a few shillings.

He had an uncle in Edinburgh and he went to live with him while he studied to improve his playing and musical knowledge. Today we would hardly even consider the possibility, but the young Duncan made his way to Edinburgh on foot, a distance of some sixty miles. At this point in the 1780s Edinburgh was a centre for all sort of things as well as being where the best Scottish musicians flocked to. The European philosophical movement known as the Enlightenment was in full stream, and nowhere more so than in Edinburgh. There were also a great many dances and balls going on in Edinburgh and dozens of dancing-masters were plying their trade. It was just the place for an aspiring young musician to improve himself, and improvement was very much the buzzword of the time in philosophy, social affairs, agriculture and the embryonic discipline of economics. After a few months of such a heady mix Samson thought he was ready to return home to Perthshire.

At this time, apart from the entertainment provided by the various types of dances, theatres were very popular. Touring groups of actors would put on selections of different types of plays, including melodrama and farce. In Perth theatrical touring shows were put on in Glover's Hall in George Street. Not long after Samson's return, a group of actors took over at Glover's Hall and the manager of the group needed an orchestra. Hearing of the skills of Samson Duncan, particularly that he could read arrangements on sight, he sought the young lad out and offered him the job of orchestra leader. At his age this was quite a notable achievement, and, given the popularity of the theatre in those days, his new position was the talk of the town and soon of the whole county. We tend to think of celebrity as a modern phenomenon but people have always found successful contemporaries glamorous.

One night, not long after his appointment as orchestra leader, the programme had just passed the melodrama and the orchestra were readying themselves to accompany the farce that followed when a voice rang out. A Kinclaven farmer had come to the theatre, full of pride that a local laddie was doing so well in the entertainment business, and couldn't contain himself any longer.

Full of rural pride, and maybe a drappie or two, he roared out, 'Samson, gie's a tune, or we'll aw gae awa hame!' This caused great hilarity in the rest of the audience and Samson was forced to take a few bows. Such incidents aside, however, the lad did well in his new position. Such was the success of the run that when the players were leaving Perth the manager of the group, delighted with the contribution from the young fiddler, asked him to go with the company at the very respectable sum of thirty shillings a week. However, Samson was still very young and thought he should consult with his father before accepting such an offer, tempting as it undoubtedly was. Now, his father was a relatively successful miller, a man used to running his own affairs, but he had no knowledge whatsoever of what life on the road for a travelling musician would be like. The offered wage was considerable but he had nothing really to compare it to. He was unsure of what to do, so he turned to another for advice.

This was Mercer, Laird of Aldie, a man of considerable wealth and some standing in the community. His family had been in Perthshire for centuries and had in fact donated significant lands to the City of Perth in the past. The family mansion was at Meiklour, a few miles north of Perth, and they were very much a part of the Scottish aristocracy at the time. Now, some will say that the advice given by Mercer was sensible and that he was doing the boy a favour. He told John Duncan that, while the salary on offer was certainly not to be sneezed at, the life of a travelling musician, like that of any other showman, was necessarily precarious and that it was most likely that the boy's morals would become corrupted. This was something that would, put the wind up any devout Presbyterian at the time and John Duncan was in a quandary. It was clear that, despite the fine wages, the job was too dangerous, but he was reluctant to deny his son the chance to make such a good salary. The upshot of it all was that Mercer offered to hire Samson as a musician at Meiklour House, a situation that seems actually to have suited everyone. However, it also puts one in mind of the old saying: 'if a laird shakes your hand, make sure you count your fingers afterwards'.

Shortly afterwards Duncan met Niel Gow at Meiklour House, where he was regular visitor. Samson was eighteen and Niel approaching sixty. The hospitality at the Mercers' home was legendary, with the punch bowl being constantly topped up. It was the scene of a great deal of conviviality and Gow himself said it was the second best house in Perthshire, reserving the first position for his patron and friend the duke of Athol at Blair Castle. Niel was impressed by the young lad and they enjoyed playing together, Samson going on to play with the great man in such places as Perth, Dundee, Aberdeen and Edinburgh. In addition, they were also invited to play at a series of balls around Inverness. Samson played these engagements without his elderly companion, who maybe thought the distance too great or perhaps just didn't fancy the tour at the time. It would hardly have been because of his age: for a great many years after he still preferred to make his own way all over Scotland on foot with a clean shirt in his bag rather than be conveyed in a carriage. It was general knowledge that, due to his walking pace and knowledge of the hills of Scotland, he often got to the appointed places before the carriages anyway!

Today we tend to think that back in the nineteenth century people lived locally and didn't get around much. However, such was the popularity of fiddle music in particular that musicians regularly travelled across the Scottish–English border in both directions and fiddlers like Niel Gow and others were well known even in such distant spots as London. Samson himself went to play in London with another Perthshire player, John Bowie, just about the turn of the nineteenth century, when the Perthshire fiddlers were highly renowned. Niel Gow was getting too old to accompany them but at the time Niel's son, John, was making a living as a fiddler in London himself. Samson and John Bowie played at several of the Perthshire nobility's private parties, as well as at some of the Highland Society's London meetings along with John Gow's band.

After the death of his father, Samson moved back to the family cottage and continued to have a relationship with the Mercers. The old laird was dead by this time and his position as the family musician was virtually an honorary one.

Increasingly finding work in Perth, Samson moved his entire family there in 1810 and took on a great many pupils, both on the fiddle and the piano. This led in time to his developing a piano business, which flourished for many years. He began to cut back on playing live engagements and eventually devoted all his time to the business, though it seems likely he might have dropped in on the odd night to the Old Ship Inn in the city's Skinnergate, which was the meeting place for Perth's musicians for many years. Before retiring from public performance he was invited to play at the Grand Ball before George IV on his tartanised visit to Edinburgh in 1822, along with Nathaniel Gow, which probably seemed a decent swansong to an illustrious career.

An Eye for the Main Chance

Even in the modern world, a musician's life can be a fragile one in terms of regular income. While there are many people who make fortunes, often with little or no discernible talent, there have always been musicians whose considerable talents have not guaranteed them a good living. Sometimes such people develop tendencies that veer from the straight and true. Poverty has a way of making people doubt the wisdom of the old saying that honesty is the best policy. One fiddler in the early nineteenth century who developed his own techniques for increasing his income was Patie Birnie from Kinghorn, who played around the shores of the Forth in the later years of the seventeenth century.

This was before dancing attained its almost universal popularity and Patie, born Patrick, like many another musician, had to ply his trade in the streets and taverns of the time. He and a pal of his, Johnny Stocks, developed an approach that preyed on the gullibility of travellers, often picking on those who were taking the ferry from Burntisland to Edinburgh. It was generally the practice of travellers awaiting the ferry to spend their time in a nearby ale-house – little has changed, really – and it was here that Patie's ploys would come into effect, at either end of the journey across the Forth. He would keep hidden out of sight till he saw what he considered a suitable target, one or more gentlemen entering the ale-house by the ferry. Once he was sure they were seated with a drink he would arrive at a rush, his fiddle under his arm, pretending to be out of breath.

'Ah, there ye are, sirs, I beg yer pardon for keeping you waiting but I am here now and will give you a spring or two,' he would sputter out, then launch into some well-known and popular tune. The bemused strangers, knowing fine they had not asked for a fiddler to entertain them, would either think he was confusing them with someone else or that the landlord had sent for him. In any case, it usually transpired that at the very least they would buy the fiddler a drink. That was enough for Patie to get into conversation and then he would attempt to milk them for all he possibly could. Even when he knew fine well that he had never seen the person before, he was liable to drop in remarks between tunes: 'Och, I weel kennt your honour's father, sir. A guid and honest man he was and we had many a drink thegither.' As the strangers were in no great hurry to get deep into conversation with the somewhat grubby and unkempt fiddler they rarely pushed him on this. Another trick he would use arose from the fact that he had quite a good ear. This served him well musically and also led to him generally being able to locate people's places of origin, if they were Scottish. He would talk of how much he liked their home town, and in truth he had travelled much of the country over the years. Patie also knew a few jokes and tall tales and was liable to drop a few of these into his performance, which usually served to earn him a few pence. He was, in short, an entertainer of his time.

If things were going well he would regale his audience with his own views of music, with references to 'cork-headed loons wha ran awa tae Italy tae learn the "hahas" of Italian music, when aw the time there was nothing to beat the auld Scotch tunes. Such Italian frippery is hardly fit for real men yer honours,' he would say, before launching into another tune, either a rollicking reel or an old and sentimental air. Patie liked to tell his pals that he might not have had the most extensive repertoire in the world but he knew what people liked.

If things were going well, his old pal Johnny Stocks, a short, powerfully-built man, who looked like a miner but who had hardly ever done an honest day's work in his life, would come in and do a bit of dancing to add to the entertainment. He would climb up onto a table and caper about, generally to great laughter, but now and again would attempt a more elegant performance with any young lass prepared to put up with him. There were instances where the performance of the fiddler and the dancer were well appreciated by a crowd of travellers and in those circumstances they would, if asked, happily accompany the group across on the ferry, whichever way it was going. They had access to beds at either end of the ferry, Patie's sister living in Kinghorn, near Burntisland, and Johnny having an extended family in Leith. As long as there was a drink and a few pennies in it they would perform anywhere. They were a pair of scallywags and if things got tight at the ferry they would simply wander off elsewhere for a while. The life of an itinerant street musician seems to have suited Patie well but he always returned to Kinghorn.

He was well known in the area and, after a particularly long series of wild and extravagant nights, ended up taking to his bed at his sister's. He was so unwell that the minister was called for and poor Patie, feeling he was at death's door, said to the man of the cloth that if he were spared he would never get drunk again.

A fortnight later the minister was walking along the quay when Patie lurched from a tavern door and almost fell over him.

'Heavens above, Birnie, look at the state of you. What about yer promise to forswear the drink?' the minister demanded.

'Ach, weel, meenister,' smiled the fiddler, 'ye should ken better than take the word o a man that's riven wi the fever.'

He was long remembered as the composer of both words and music for the tune 'The Auld Man's Mare's Dead', which remained a favourite long after his death.

When the Muse Strikes

One evening in the 1890s a group of fiddlers met up in a pub in Dumfries. During a break in the playing, as fresh drinks were brought to their table, the talk turned to great fiddlers of the past.

'Och, there nivver was oniebodie that was as great as Niel Gow,' said Davie Duncan, a local ploughman. 'That 'Farewell tae Whisky' is just braw.'

'Aye, he certainly was a grand composer,' nodded Archie Holton, a butcher in the town and, at nearly fifty, the oldest of the five fiddlers there. 'But for masel I mind my grandfaither tellin me that he thought the best he ever heard was William Marshal fae up Aberdeen way. I've a collection or two o his tunes an they tak some beatin.'

'Well, what about players the day?' put in Martin Barr, a wee stout man in his thirties, who worked as a carrier all over Dumfries and Galloway. 'I've heard that Scott Skinner three or fower times now an I reckon he is as good as oniebodie that has ever put horsehair tae catgut,' the little man said.

'That's as may be,' interjected Lang Tam Lewis, a ploughman on a nearby farm and a man who stood six foot six inches in his stocking soles, 'but we should nivver forget our ain folk. Ye'll aw pardon me if I pit forward the name o a local man, and a plooman forbye.' At this he stopped and smiled. Smiles were returned by the men who had already spoken and all nodded.

The fifth member of the company was John McNairn, a clerk at the County Court, who had only moved into the district a few weeks before. This was only his second time meeting with the local fiddlers and he had no idea who they were talking about.

'A local player? An who would that be?' he asked.

'In the name o some big hoose,' Barr exploded, 'are ye seriously telling me ye have nivver heard o Johnstone o Turnmuir?'

'Well, no, I cannae say I have ever heard of him,' said McNairn, a bit taken aback at the vehemence with which Barr had spoken. 'Is he a local?'

At this Holton gave a laugh. 'Weel, ye could say he is.' He paused.

'An on the ither hand,' Duncan put in, 'ye could say he isnae.'

The four local men all laughed, taking good-natured pleasure in the look of bemusement on McNairn's features.

'I don't understand. How can he be local an no local?' he asked of the company in general.

'Ach, well,' said Holton, 'we're jist pullin yer leg, Johnnie. He was local but he's been deid these fifty years an more.'

'I've heard he's buried doun near Annan so he's still local enough.' Duncan added with a smile.

'He was a grand fiddler then?' asked McNairn, smiling to show he understood the joke.

'And a ploughman forbye,' added Lewis.

'Aye, he was said tae have been ane o the very best,' Holton continued, 'an Lang Tam's right enough for he was a ploughman himself. It seems he worked on his faither's farm, but he surely had an eccentric way o working.'

He paused and McNairn noticed that the other three fiddlers had sat back in their chairs, knowing the story to come. They had heard it a thousand times before but still it could do with another telling.

The old butcher went on with the story, picking up a glass of beer from the tray that had just been put on the table by the bonny young lass McNairn had noticed earlier. Now though, his attention was on the story the old fiddler was telling him.

'Ye see, he had been a keen fiddler since he was only five or six and he liked naethin more nor composin tunes. His father was driven near daft with his cantrips. He used to put his fiddle on a string ower his back when he was ploughin in the fields, just in case a thought or a new tune came to him while he was workin, an it seems that he was aye composin – he could hardly stop himsel. The horse would stand happily enough when he stopped to dash off a phrase or two. So ye can see that he was aye behind wi the work his faither set him. So the old fella eventually banned him from takkin his fiddle tae the fields. They had a richt old argie-bargie about it, but the young fella could hardly deny that he wisnae pullin his weight.

'Anyway, a week or so later Auld Johnstone had tae head down here to the toun tae see about some cattle he was wantin to buy. He had a good day an settled things wi the farmer he had met and they had a dram or so tae seal their bargain. So, as ye can imagine, the auld fairmer was feelin pretty pleased wi himsel as he came home on the wee cart he used to travel about on. He had just come on his own land and turned a corner past a wee copse o trees beside the field where his son was workin – weel, where he was supposed tae be workin. The first thing he sees is the plough team are at a standstill. He starts cursin an yellin at the lad for brakkin his word an takkin his fiddle tae the field, an he runs into the field. He gets up tae the team an there they are wi the reins draggin in the mud. But there's nae a sign o oor fiddler.

'He'd been struck by a musical thought an, no haein his fiddle on his back, what had he done? Why, he just legged it straight back tae the farmhouse, over a mile away, hummin the snatch at the top o his voice as he ran. Ye can imagine the words when the farmer got hame. His anger didnae last long when he heard the new tune his laddie had written, though. It wisnae long after that that they hired a new ploughman on Turnmuir farm and Johnstone went off tae play full time, wi the auld man's blessin. There's times when ye cannae stand in the way o what must be.'

This last statement was met with nods and grunts of approval, as glasses were downed, fiddles taken up. Once more the night rang with the sound of good Scots fiddles that night in Dumfries. And quite a few of the tunes played had been composed on the fiddle of Johnston of Turnmuir.

Peter Milne

Fiddlers, like other musicians, develop deep feelings for their instruments. Down the years many a wife has complained that her musician husband has lavished more care and attention on his instrument than he has on her, and justifiably so in more than a few cases. One man who dearly loved his fiddle was Peter Milne, known as the Torland Minstrel. Peter was born in Kincardine O'Neil in 1824 and originally worked as a cowherd on nearby farms. He had an ear for music from an early age; he saved up his meagre wages, bought a fiddle and taught himself to play – by the time-honoured and still viable process of watching and listening to other fiddlers. Though there are always those miserable souls who try to keep what they know to themselves and resent people learning from them, most traditional musicians have always been happy to help others learn, so Peter got on fine. In fact he got on so well that by the age of seventeen he was playing in the orchestra at Aberdeen's Theatre Royal. In 1851 he became the leader of the orchestra there, succeeding James Young. He supplemented his income by playing at halls and barn dances around Aberdeenshire, particularly on Deeside. In 1862, like many others before him, Milne moved to Edinburgh to further his career and successfully led orchestras at the Princess and Gaiety Theatres. He also had the chance to tour England on several occasions. However, he fell victim to the musician's curse of rheumatism in the fingers and as a result became addicted to laudanum, a derivative of opium that was freely available in Victorian times. The limitations of his condition, and perhaps the side-effects of a laudanum habit, seem to have caused him some problems. In his later years we hear of him playing on the ferries that ran between Fife and Leith across the Forth – a bit of a comedown for a one-time orchestra leader.

However, he then went back home and found support on his own patch, giving concerts in and around his adopted home town of Tarland before landing a job in the Alhambra Theatre in Aberdeen. He had some sort of accident in 1898 and, for the last ten years of his life, Peter was unable to work and was forced to live in poverty – no welfare state was in existence then. Although in many ways representative of fiddlers of his time, Peter is best remembered for an odd saying. He was prone to tell people: 'I am that fond of my fiddle that I could go inside her and look out.' In the course of his varied career in Aberdeen, Edinburgh and elsewhere, Peter played with many of the country's finest musicians and was instrumental in helping Scott Skinner to further both his talent and his career. In 1852 the young Skinner joined him in Aberdeen at the Theatre Royal and they played together off and on for the next ten years.

Scott Skinner

Just as Niel Gow was the most famous Scottish fiddler of the eighteenth century, the nineteenth century saw the rise of James Scott Skinner. Born at Banchory in 1843, his father and elder brother both played the fiddle. His brother Sandy also played cello and taught both instruments to James. His father was a fair

violinist and a well-respected dancing master. He was a remarkable man in his own right. In those far off days it was the custom
at country weddings for the men to shoot their guns in the air, as
still happens in many parts of the world today. This is dangerous
anywhere, and the situation in Scotland was of course made that
bit more risky by the intake of whisky. Weddings have long been
seen as an excuse for a 'good drink', but then again so have
funerals, baptisms and many other social occasions. At one
wedding, however, William was a bit more fou than he should
have been and, in the course of firing his own gun, took off a
couple of fingers on his left hand. This was pretty dreadful for a
fiddler, but William Skinner was made of strong stuff. He decided
the only thing to do in the circumstances was to give up his job
as a gardener and to become a full-time dancing master. This
allowed him the time to change his way of playing and pretty
soon he was as proficient left-handed as he had been right-
handed! He was successful enough to raise a large family, none
of whom ever knew poverty in their childhood.

So it was into a comfortable and musical family that James
Scott Skinner was born in Banchory, Aberdeenshire, on
5 August 1843. With both his father and elder brother Sandy
being musicians, he was off to a good start. Sandy had been out
playing with their father from an early age and soon taught the
young James both fiddle and cello, an instrument on which
Sandy had long been accompanying their father. James was also
fortunate in having lessons with Peter Milne, a noted player and
teacher, who lived in Aboyne. Peter was the leader of the
orchestra at Aberdeen's Theatre Royal in the 1850s, and well
known as both a fiddler and a composer. Musically, James
showed himself to be a keen pupil and by the age of eight he was
playing cello with Milne, whom Skinner later claimed was
'practically a father to me'.

The life of a musician was not easy and for the young Skinner
it must have been particularly tough. In his autobiography he

mentioned that it was not unusual for them to have to walk as much as ten miles in the slushy dampness of a Scottish winter's night to play at a barn dance. Here, in his own words, is a description of his return from one such engagement:

> I remember getting back from such a tramp about five o'clock in the morning. So tired was I that when I got to the door dragging, rather than carrying, my bass fiddle, I had neither the strength nor the willpower to lift the latch and enter. I must have been in a subconscious state, for when my mother opened the door about seven I fell right through the doorway, and lay helpless at her feet. I had been sleeping against the door, in a half-standing, half-leaning posture for two hours at least.

So, with the help of Milne, James was off playing with his father and brothers at bothy dances, weddings and other social occasions before the age of ten.

Having shown himself to be a good reader as well as fine player, he was picked up by the touring show, 'Dr Mark's Little Men'. This was a group of boy musicians, supposedly all orphans, who played in theatres and music halls. Their repertoire was composed of light classical music. While in the orchestra, based in Manchester, James studied with the violinist Charles Rougier, who was famous throughout Europe. This improved his technique and general musical skills and, in all, Skinner spent six years with the group travelling all over the United Kingdom, laying a solid basis for the excellent showman he was eventually to become. Once while in London the orchestra performed before Queen Victoria at Buckingham Palace; earlier that same day Scott Skinner had been busking for money in the streets of the capital.

After a brief interlude as a blackface minstrel, James Scott Skinner began his career as concert violinist in earnest. At twenty,

James entered a competition in Inverness and beat the very best of contemporary Scottish fiddlers. His vigorous attack and superb bowing made him stand out. From then on he never looked back. Calling himself 'The Strathspey King', he toured Scotland, England and then America and Canada, where the expatriate Scottish communities welcomed him with open arms.

Skinner ended up playing to vast audiences at London's Palladium and Royal Albert Hall, usually dressed in a kilt. He was completely subsumed in a presentation of Scottish culture that nowadays we see as kitsch. But it was the very embodiment of the romantic Victorian version of traditional Highland culture, and achieved great and lasting success. His travels to America and Canada set a pattern for many Scottish musicians that continues today, with audiences there and in Australia and New Zealand ever eager for Scottish music. This romantic vision of the Scottish Highlander was almost entirely an invention of the late eighteenth and early nineteenth centuries and coincided with the creation of great Highland hunting estates that were much more feudal than anything that had ever existed in the Highlands before.

Skinner toured concert-shows that included dancers and singers and, though the repertoire was rooted in the reels, strathspeys, airs and pastorals that he had known since childhood, there is no doubt he had moved on considerably from his early days at bothy dances and country weddings. He published several collections of his own compositions, which were snapped up by fiddlers of all levels; some of his tunes are still being played today.

However, he didn't always have it easy and lost considerable amounts of money at various times. One time, when he wasn't doing too well, he was lying in his bed thinking of the generosity of his friend William McHardy, who was affectionately known as the Laird o Drumblair, after the estate he had bought on returning to Scotland. A successful engineer, who had made a small fortune in South America, McHardy had been generous in his support for the fiddler. As he lay there thinking, a new Strathspey popped up in his head. Immediately, he looked for paper to write it down. There was none to hand – things had been tight for a while – so he picked up a piece of soap wrapping, flattened it out and proceeded to write out the tune. On informing his wife that he was sending this off to McHardy, she replied, 'Ye're no' gaun tae send that awfy-like paper tae the Laird. He'll jist licht his pipe wi'it!'

Send it he did, however, and was duly rewarded the following Christmas with a letter of gratitude and accompanying cheque. And the cheques arrived every Christmas thereafter.

David Rizzio and James Oswald

David Rizzio or Riccio, an Italian musician, is at the heart of one of the most scandalous episodes in Scottish history, stabbed to death in front of Mary Queen of Scots by her then husband, Lord Darnley. Biographers of Mary have stated that Rizzio was the composer of several well-known Scottish tunes, including the 'Lass o Patie's Mill'. The truth would appear to be somewhat different. In an anonymous painting of David Rizzio, painted after his death but possibly based on an earlier portrait, he is shown holding what appears to be a viol. It is like a modern violin but appears to have at least five strings; as the head is unclear, we don't know how many pegs it had. That Rizzio was a musician is certain. He had come to Scotland in 1561 as part of the retinue of the Italian nobleman, Count Robertino Solara di Moreta, the ambassador from Savoy. Rizzio was a sophisticated, widely-travelled man and an accomplished musician. It was in fact his singing skills that first drew the attention of the queen. Mary was very fond of music and, having spent much of her life in France, she brought viol players with her on her return. At this time the rebec and the fithel were still popular in Scotland; there is a report from a visiting Frenchman of a crowd of three hundred

Edinburgh citizens coming to Holyrood to serenade the queen with psalm-singing, accompanied by rebecs and other stringed instruments. According to his account, the performance was severely out of tune but the supposedly arch-Puritan John Knox, never a friend of Mary, wrote that it had pleased the queen and that she asked for it to be repeated for several nights.

When the Savoyard ambassador returned to Italy, Mary was short of a bass singer for her chapel quartet; she asked if Rizzio, a baritone, could stay behind and sing for her. He was then appointed as valet de chambre on an annual salary of twenty pounds. By 1564 he had been appointed Mary's foreign secretary, in charge of her correspondence abroad. Being a Catholic and free of any of the dominant Scottish Presbyterianism of the time, he soon became a favourite of Mary's. There was a great deal of political intrigue going on and Rizzio unwittingly found himself at the heart of it. As a foreigner and a Catholic, he was a figure of suspicion to many of the Scots nobles and particularly to Mary's husband, the foppish and petulant Lord Darnley. Despite the reservations of many of the nobles, Mary spent an increasing amount of time with Rizzio and rumours soon started that they were having an affair. Even Mary's illegitimate half-brother, the earl of Moray, came to loathe Rizzio and his supposed influence over his sister. The upshot of all this was a plot to get rid of the Italian musician. Darnley, who was generally despised for his scandalous behaviour in Edinburgh's taverns and brothels, grew increasingly angry at the relationship between his wife, who had effectively spurned him, and her secretary. It all came to a head on 19 March 1566 when, with Darnley's support, Rizzio was murdered in front of the queen in her private apartment in Holyrood palace. The unfortunate Italian was stabbed a total of fifty-six times. It was a brutal and despicable act in front of a woman who was then seven months pregnant with the future James VI of Scotland and I of England. In later years the site of the murder became something of a tourist attraction, with the supposed bloodstains on the floor being repainted again and again.

However, the idea that this talented Italian musician contributed to the repertoire of Scottish song is a dubious one. In the early part of the eighteenth century there was a talented fiddler and dancing master in Edinburgh called James Oswald. He composed a considerable number of tunes, many of which were extremely popular at the time. For a while he used the pen-name David Rizzio. Oswald was also a singer and a promoter of concerts in the city and, although he moved to London in 1741, he went on to publish the Caledonian Pocket Companion in fifteen volumes between 1747 and 1769. He was no doubt aware of the story of the Rizzio assassination and its continuing public attraction through the repainting of the murder scene; he either had a sense of humour or saw some sort of publicity opportunity in adopting such a nom-de-plume. It would seem clear that the tunes attributed to the unfortunate sixteenth-century Italian were actually composed by a native of Edinburgh in the eighteenth century.

Fiddler Tam

The seventh earl of Kellie was quite a notable figure in the mid-eighteenth century. Despite his aristocratic background and breeding, he was a true Scot – like Niel Gow he was at home with all levels of contemporary society, from humble cottar's turf-built home to the great palaces of the nation. Like Gow, he also was a fiddler and the common people of West Fife where he was raised came to know him as Fiddler Tam. Born in 1732, he was the first son of the sixth earl of Kellie and was raised with distinct Jacobite tendencies. His father had joined up with Charles Edward Stuart in his rebellion and, after the bloody end of that fatal adventure at Drumossie Moor on the 16 April 1746, he found himself imprisoned.

The earl escaped the gallows but was locked up in Edinburgh jail till 1749. While he awaited release, his wife was trying to prove that he was insane! While he wasn't clinically insane, he was, like his son, a bit eccentric. Just before being released from Edinburgh castle, he went into a room in the castle to tell his fellow prisoners who was to be released. There must have been several there whose hearts were in their mouths, waiting to see if they were to be let free. As the leading aristocrat there, his name was, according to the custom of the time, at the head of the list. The earl, his sense of humour undimmed by his incarceration, glanced down to see who was the final name on the list. Seeing this, he snorted, then announced to the assembled company: 'Here we are, lads, a list fae the government an ye cannae think they're wise. They start their list wi a fool an finish wi a fiddler.' He meant that he himself was the fool and the last man named was a Mr Fiddler, which, given his son's musical talents, seems somewhat prophetic!

His son Thomas, the sixth earl of Kellie, grew up to be one of Scotland's finest composers, his own favourite instrument being the violin. His music within the classical tradition was known well beyond Scotland in his lifetime and he was considered to be a composer of considerable talent. However, while capable of writing music that delighted the polite society of eighteenth-century Scotland, Fiddler Tam was also a frequent visitor to the inns and taverns of the East Neuk of Fife. He was a fine violinist in the Scottish tradition, had a good strong bowing hand and took great delight in playing Scottish music. His skills made him pleasant company. He cared not one bit who he was with as long as the music and the claret ran free. It was as a result of his open-hearted conviviality that he was given his nickname by his tenants and others in the East Neuk. It seems that, away from the music of the drawing room in polite society, he liked little more than to spend his evenings in the hostelries of the area, drinking and playing music with the common folk. No doubt his relative wealth made him very popular with the denizens of the East Neuk hostelries of the time.

In his later years his pleasure-seeking told on his appearance. His face was extremely florid and was often studded with pimples, caused by an over-enthusiastic love of the bottle and the resultant effects on his liver. In fact, one wag, when Thomas visited him one day, took him out into his garden and, referring to his guest's high colour, said, 'Pray, my Lord, look over that wall there upon my cucumber bed. It has had no sun to speak of at all yet this year.' We do not know what Thomas's reply was but it seems likely that he took the joke in good part. He died without an heir in Brussels and was succeeded by his brother, who only outlived him by a few years, passing away in 1797. The direct line of the Kellies was at an end and it nearly did end with a fiddler. The title moved to a distant cousin, as such things usually do.

Rascality Indeed!

We have seen that even great musicians like Niel Gow were not perhaps the best of technical players and that sight-reading was not always necessary to be able to play the fiddle. There has long been argument about whether being able to sight-read makes someone a better musician – after all, many highly trained classical players are incapable of improvising a note, while many non-readers are happy to do nothing but improvise. Maybe the truth is that while sight-reading is not an absolute necessity, it certainly can have many advantages.

Traditional music, while conforming to specific melodic or chordal structures, tends to be in only a handful of keys, which are generally the easiest in which to play them on the violin. 'Classical' music tends to be more complex and played in a greater variety of keys, partially to suit more complicated instrumentation. There is a story about a weel-kennt fiddler from

Longside, near Peterhead, called Jamie Duncan that illustrates the differing attitudes towards music. Jamie was known as a man who was not only a first-class sight-reader but could play his repertoire in virtually any key. One evening at a dance, things had been going well when the second fiddler stopped playing, stuck his fiddle in his bag and stomped off stage. He went straight to the door of the hall without a backward look.

The fellow on the door had seen what happened and asked, 'What's wrong, man? What for have ye stopped playin?'

The fiddler drew himself up to his full height, his whiskers bristling, and burst out, 'I hae kept decent company aw my days and I'm in nae mind tae change now. That Jamie Duncan – ' and he pointed angrily up at the stage where Jamie was playing happily on – 'That Jamie Duncan is now playin 'Monymusk' in four flats, an I say that onie man that would dae that is capable o aw sorts o rascality. Guid nicht.' And with that the fiddler stomped off, never to play with Jamie Duncan again!

Otherworld Tales

⟫◦◦◦⟪

The supernatural plays a strong part in all storytelling traditions, so it is little wonder that in Scotland we have so many stories of fairies luring fiddlers away. Variants mention pipers and other musicians in different local traditions. Basically, the story is that a couple of musicians are on their way home from a wedding or other social event, when they come upon a fairy hill with its door wide open. The fairies invite them in and get them to play throughout the night, plying them with high-quality whisky. In the morning they are sent on their way to find themselves in a world totally unlike the one they had left; in some cases they are said to have been in the fairy hill for a century or more. Once they realise what has happened, they usually crumble away to dust. Variants of this story continue to be told with some versions having the fiddlers coming across motorcars in the streets of a modern town or city when all they knew was horse transport. Apart from showing that stories, no matter how ancient, can continue to reinvent themselves for a changing audience, there are other aspects of this kind of story that are intriguing. Professor Ron Hutton in his book *Pagan Religions in the Ancient British Isles* talks of a similar group of stories that involve sleeping warriors, usually led by King Arthur or Finn MacCoul in Scotland, resting inside significant hills. Hutton suggested that this is in fact a memory from the time the chambered cairns were built, as long as 5,000 years ago. Most of these great massive communal graves were raised in the period 2000–3500 BC, but in some cases even earlier. Hutton suggests that, as we know that the remains of a great many people were kept together, in the form of skulls and thigh bones, the mounds were probably the scene of rites, where religious practitioners, akin to shamans or druids, would attempt to commune with the spirits of the dead ancestors, represented by the bones, to ask their help in ensuring fertility for the coming year. The ancestors, whose remains other than skulls and tibia had probably been burnt and scattered on the ground or buried, were asked to work their influence – or magic – on the planted seeds to ensure crops for the coming year. It seems at least possible that the fiddlers in the fairy mound stories are part of the same type of memory – fairy mounds in local stories often turn out to be burial mounds, just as the hollow hills where Arthur and Finn MacCoul lie sleeping with their warriors tend to be hills associated with the old communal fire festivals of Beltane (1 May), and Samhain (Halloween). If there is anything to this suggestion, the type of instrument played by the musicians in the stories has probably changed over the hundreds and hundreds of years these stories have been told. It does, however, underline that the fiddle is an integral part of Scottish culture and has been for some considerable time.

We couldn't have a section of supernatural tales without mention of the devil, who in Scotland has long been familiarly known as Auld Clootie, Auld Hornie or Auld Nick, as if he was a distant uncle to us all.

The Fiddler o Gord

In Orkney traditional lore there are creatures known as trowes, the same kind of otherworldly beings as the Scandinavian trolls, reflecting the strong Norse aspects of local culture. These trowes were generally malignant creatures, bigger and more bloodthirsty than even the worst of the fairies, and many stories were told of them. Like other similar creatures, they were believed to inhabit knowes or mounds, many of which were in fact the burial mounds of ancient times.

At Sandness, near Papa Stour in Orkney, there was a crofter who lived near the sea with his wife and children. Like crofters through the ages, he combined working a small plot of land with harvesting the sea; to help feed his growing family he would regularly go down to the shore to fish for sillocks off the rocks. One time he was on his way back to his cottage just after dark with a fine bundle of sillocks when he noticed something strange. One of the knowes near the beach seemed to have a light shining from within it. He could hear music from inside and, being a keen fiddler himself, he was intrigued by the music, which was unlike any he had ever heard before. So, putting down his fish, he went closer and looked in. There was a strange sight indeed. The local trowes were having a dance, the music being played on a beautiful old fiddle by a fearsome-looking creature. Totally entranced by the eerie music, he went in, not noticing as the door closed silently behind him.

When he hadn't returned by the morning, his wife was beside herself with worry and a search party was put together from amongst the neighbours, none of whom lived that close. They scoured the shore and the area behind it, but not a sign of the crofter could be found. After a whole day's searching, the sorry conclusion was reached that he must have been swept off the rocks by a freak wave while fishing. It was well known that every ninth wave was much stronger than the rest, and people thought he must not have been paying attention when the big wave came. His family were distraught and life became even harder for his wife and her children. However, she worked hard and the children grew up healthy. As they grew to adulthood they all thought to move away – there were far more opportunities in the towns of Orkney and maybe even the mainland. The tragedy of their father's disappearance hung heavy in all their hearts, and, much though they loved their home, there were constant reminders of their lost father. So, one after another they left; at last the day came when the crofter's wife too moved away, to live with one of her sons in the town of Stromness. Another family moved into the cottage and the years passed. Eventually, a new century came in.

One night in the heart of winter the grandfather of the new family, who had lived all his days in the cottage, was sitting by the fire, his son and his wife beside him and a wee crowd of bonny bairns playing around their feet. The night was wild and the famous Orkney wind was blowing up a storm. Suddenly, the door of the cottage flew open. There stood an old man with a long white beard, dressed in rags and clutching an ancient-looking fiddle in his right hand. The children laughed in surprise at this sudden vision, and their parents rose to their feet at the sight of the stranger. One of the children, Jamie, the oldest and nearly twelve years old, who was learning to play the fiddle, hadn't laughed; he was looking intently at the old instrument in the stranger's hands.

The stranger spoke. 'What are you all doing in my house?'

'Och, he's soft in the head, probably just an old tramp,' the wife whispered to her man.

The man repeated his question, and the children began laughing again.

'Wheesht,' said the grandfather, still sitting by the fire. 'Come over here by the fire and warm yourself, sir.'

The stranger moved to the fire, a wild look in his eyes, and gingerly sat down, nervously looking around him. Again he said that this was his house, but that it seemed different to him.

'What is your name?' asked the grandfather.

'I am Allan Jamieson, and this is my home. Where are my wife and bairns?' the stranger replied, his voice catching in his throat.

'Allan Jamieson,' mused the grandfather, 'I know the name. My grandfather told me there was a family here in the old times called Jamieson and that the father disappeared one evening and was never seen again.'

'When was this?' gasped the white-haired old stranger.

'Och, it would be a hundred years ago now,' replied the grandfather.

'A hundred years, oh my God,' sobbed the stranger. 'And what of my wife, my bairns?'

'Och, well, they all moved away to the towns, but I'm afraid they'll all be long dead by now,' the old man said softly.

'Dead. All dead,' the stranger repeated, trembling with sorrow. Then he sighed, gave himself a shake and stood up. 'I thank you sir, but I think it time I went to join my family.' And he moved to the door.

They all sat and watched as the ancient stranger left – all except for Jamie, who followed the strange old man out into the night. No one had noticed, but the wind had dropped and the fairy dancers, the Northern Lights, streaked the winter sky. Jamie stood and watched as the stranger walked to the bottom of the cottage garden. There he raised the fiddle and played a strange and eerie tune. He finished the tune and started it again. This time, as he finished, the fiddle fell from his hands and he collapsed to the ground. Jamie ran forward. There, lying on the ground, was nothing but a skeleton with scraps of rags attached to it, and lying beside it an ancient fiddle, which, as he reached to pick it up, crumbled to dust before his eyes. But he always remembered the tune that Jamieson had learned from the trolls and, if asked often enough, would even play it in the long midwinter nights at Sandness.

With the Fairies' Help

There are tales told all over Scotland of how people suffered by being lured into the fairy mounds. Such tales exist in the north and the south and the east and west and rarely do the people concerned meet anything but a sad end. However, there were once two young men in Lewis who met the fairies to no disadvantage at all. They were out late one night when they saw a green light shining out from a fairy knoll. They stood still in astonishment, hardly aware of what was happening to them, till they realised they were listening to a fairy orchestra, playing within the mound. One of them, Jamie, was a keen young fiddler and he had never heard such fine playing as was coming from the mound. He started to go towards it.

'No, no, Jamie, ye cannae go in there – ye'll be enchanted and the fairies'll never let ye go,' his pal Dougal pleaded with him.

But Jamie's mind was made up – he was entranced by the music and, shrugging off Dougal's attempts to hold him back, he headed into the knoll. As soon as he went inside, the entrance closed up and the green fairy light shone no more. Poor Dougal was left the sad task of going back to the village and telling Jamie's parents that their son had gone off with the fairies. Over the next few months quite a few of the villagers kept their distance from Dougal; they wanted nothing to do with anyone who had any involvement with the fairies, even vaguely.

Meanwhile, Jamie had found himself at a merry dance; when the fairies found out he was a fiddler an instrument was found for him, and he joined in happily with the music. He had a grand time playing with the fairies and, after what he thought was a few hours, he said he wanted to get back. No one made any attempt to stop him and he went out into the clear night air.

Imagine his consternation when he got back to his parents' house to find that not only had he been away for a year and a day, but his family, mother and father, brothers and sisters had all assumed he was gone forever and had given him up for dead.

Well, that night there was such a ceilidh in the house! When Jamie took up his own fiddle that he had not touched for that year and a day, the music that flew from his fingers astounded his family and the neighbours who had come in to celebrate his return. Soon his skill as a musician was talked about all over the island. Such was his artistry that no one ever doubted that he had spent all that time playing with a fairy orchestra.

The Laddie who Played for the Dance of the Fish

It wasn't that long ago a tale was told in Lewis of the Fishes' Dance. This was a magical event and rarely seen by anyone other than the musician who accompanied the dance. One time, however, an old sailor from Coll near Stornoway was out late one night. It was a bright moonlit night and the reflection of the full moon on the water glinted like a silver path. He had been working late on his croft and had gone down to the beach to sit and enjoy the beautiful quiet night. The sea was a calm as a millpond, with tiny wavelets lapping the shore like quiet laughter; there was not a breath of wind in the night air, which seemed electric with happiness. On nights like this he would sometimes come and sit on the shore and remember far-off places he had visited while he was sailing the seven seas. He was sitting looking idly at the silver track of the moon on the sea when he began to realise that it was not the moon's reflection he was seeing, but thousands upon thousands of fish.

Then the sea began to boil as the fish came out of the water and up onto the shore. As he looked open-mouthed, he saw that the great procession was headed by basking sharks and whales, then porpoises and cod, all walking on their fins and ranked two by two, swaying in a regular rhythm. Behind them came a swirling throng of smaller fishes, with sillock, herring and plaice all upright on their tailfins, coming to the beach. Just then a fiddle sprang into life; he turned to see where the sound was coming from. There, at the far end of the beach, was a wee boy playing – a wee barefoot local lad he had seen about often enough. There he sat playing on his father's fiddle like a mature musician. The old sailor could only sit, stunned, as the fish began to dance along the beach. The gentle rippling of the sea and the wonderful sound of the fiddle put him in mind of the sounds of wind in the trees, leaves drifting to the earth, the rippling of hillside burns or the gentle crackling of frosted snow underfoot. The only word that he could find to describe it was magic – pure magic. And there he sat as the fish danced jigs and reels, schottisches and cotillions, to the playing of the wee lad. It seemed to the old sailor that the night went on and on for days, as if he were entranced and spell-bound. After several hours the fish went back into the sea, just before the moon faded from the sky, and the wee lad headed home to his own bed. It was many, many years before the old sailor told anyone else about what he had seen and he knew, as others did before him, that to see such a sight was a great privilege indeed. And, like the others who had been given this blessing, he knew that for as long as the fish were dancing he had been somehow out of time, transported to a land of magic where time itself stood still.

A Fairy Wedding

Playing music for the fairies didn't always end up in tragedy; sometimes benefit could come from it, though as in all dealings with the fairies there was the need to be extremely careful. One time a young woman on the Shetland isle of Fetlar went off from her house to collect some peats for the fire. When she hadn't returned by the time of the evening meal, her husband and some others went to look for her. They went to the peats to look for her and found her lying there, dead. There was no sign of foul play, and she was buried in the local churchyard. Although it was a tragedy for her husband and her young family, people were used to the harsh realities of life and soon, outside her immediate family, her death was just accepted as 'one of those things'.

Not long after this happened, the local fiddler, Bobbie Greer, went off with his fiddle to play at a wedding. The wedding was quite a long way off, but such was his reputation as a fiddler that he was often asked to play all over the island and sometimes on other islands. To make sure that he would get to the wedding on time he got up in the middle of the night and headed off for his gig. It was a bright moonlit night. Not far on his way he met a man on the road; this seemed unusual, so he stopped to speak to him.

'A good night to you, sir,' he said.

'Aye, it's a fair night right enough,' replied the stranger. 'And where are you off to with your fiddle under your arm?'

'Och, I'm off to play at a wedding at the other side of the island and I want to get there in plenty of time,' Bobbie said, noticing that the stranger was expensively, if a little strangely, dressed. In the dark he couldn't be sure, but it seemed as if his clothes were mainly red and green.

'Well,' the stranger said with a smile, 'I am looking for a fiddler myself for a wedding this very night. I tell you what, if I make sure you are in plenty time for the other one, will you come with me now and play us a few tunes?'

Willie was bit reluctant, for by now he had realised that the man was almost certainly one of the fairy folk. But the stranger assured him he would be well rewarded so he gave in and went along with him.

'Good, good, that's grand,' the stranger said. 'Now, there's a couple of things I have to tell you about this wedding. You must be sure not to eat or drink anything while you're there, except what I give you myself. Is that all right?'

At this point Jamie was sure his suspicions were absolutely right: the man was certainly one of the People of Peace. But he was intrigued and agreed to do as the man said.

So they set off and soon they came to a great old hall, which Jamie couldn't recollect having seen before, even though he was only a few miles from his home. In they went and, sure enough, there was a crowd of people and tables full of grand-looking food with great bowls of what appeared to be punch and the odd barrel of peatreek. The stranger showed him to a seat by the wall furthest from the door into the big room and Willie sat down and began to tune up.

At that point there was commotion at the entrance and in came the bride and groom.

Who should the bride be but the woman who had died at the peats the week before! Willie recognised her and tried to catch her eye as he began playing. The crowd began to dance; as she whirled past him he looked her straight in the eye and winked – but she didn't seem to recognise him at all. He knew fine well that he was at some kind of fairy wedding, but somehow he still trusted the man he had met on the road. So he played on and soon the party was in full swing. Again and again he tried to attract the attention of the new bride, but she clearly didn't know him. And, just as at a human wedding, her attention seemed pretty fixed on the groom!

After a couple of hours the man came up to him and said,' Well, it's time to go now and I'll see you out.'

They went to the door of the hall and down the road a little bit. Then the stranger took Willie by the arm and said, 'Now, here's your fee. You played very well and I am delighted with your performance. Now, though, I want you to do something for yourself. Will you trust me?'

Willie looked at the fairy man.

'Well, you have done me no ill till now,' he said.

'Good, good. Now, you must never tell anyone where you have been this night. Never. All right?'

Willie nodded.

'Right. Well then, you take this money and go buy yourself a cow. That cow will give you two calves every year and soon you will have a full byre and be able to sell a lot of milk and cheese.'

The fiddler said, 'Well, thank you, I will certainly try that.'

'Fine, fine,' said the man, 'but remember: do not tell a soul or all your cattle will disappear.' Willie headed on his way; after only a few steps he turned round to see where his companion had gone. There was no sign of him, or of the great hall that he had been playing in with such gusto just a few minutes before. Anyway, on he went to the wedding he had been hired to play at and, despite having played for several hours already and having walked a good distance, he played fine. A glass or two of whisky set him up just nicely and the families of the bride and groom were so pleased with his playing that he got a bit of a bonus on top of his fee, as well as a fair few drinks at the end of the night. So by the time he got home he was a bit fuddled, even after all the walking, and had to sleep it off.

However, when he woke in the afternoon of the next-again day he remembered everything the fairy had said and resolved to do exactly as he had said he would. He bought himself a cow, a good steady milker, and the very first year she gave him a pair of fine healthy calves. The next year she did the same and after a few seasons he had a byre full of fine, healthy cows, all giving him a grand supply of milk. He had become quite prosperous, though looking after all those cows meant he wasn't fiddling quite as much as he had been before. He and his wife, though, were getting on well and she was pleased with his level of prosperity. A few children came along and all in all he reckoned he was doing well.

That is, until one night when yet again he had been asked to play at a wedding, this time in his own village. The groom was the son of one of his oldest friends and he played up a storm. Through being almost one of the family, the fiddler's drouth was well taken care of that night. In fact, by the time he and his wife got home he was fou, and then some.

'Well then, Meg,' he said, 'I'll just have a last dram before bed. What about yourself?'

'Och, why not,' she replied. 'It's not as if we can't afford it, eh? We're doing well these days.'

'Aye, and it's all because of this old fiddle, you know.'

'What do you mean, it's all because of your old fiddle? What are you havering about, man?'

So, well-fired up with the whisky, Willie proceeded to tell her the story of what had happened years earlier. But just as he got to the point of telling her that the fairy man had sworn him to silence he had a terrible thought.

'Oh, my God,' he shouted, leaping to his feet and running out of the house.

Meg followed, confused by what was happening. She caught up with him just as he opened the door to the byre. It was empty. All of his cows, including the original old heifer, were gone, never to be seen again.

With his cows gone, Willie Greer was a much poorer man, but luckily his fiddling skills were intact, though from that time on, whenever he had had a glass of whisky, he would tell whatever company he was in: 'You must always take care of the fairy gifts – they are fragile things indeed.'

Another Gift Story

Willie Clarke was a fiddler who played all over Shetland. One night, after a wedding, he was heading back home in the middle of the night when he passed a small hill – there are no real hills in Shetland – called the Knowe. He heard loud laughter and singing and went to investigate. The following morning his wife awoke alone. Thinking that Willie had simply stayed on to carry on the party at the wedding, as he had done so often before, or was sleeping off the effects of the drink, despite her telling him to always try and get back home as soon as possible, she thought nothing much about it. It certainly wasn't the first time this had happened. By nightfall, however, she began to worry and sent word to the township where the wedding had been held, asking where Willie was. Word soon came back that he had left the wedding and headed home on the night of the wedding! By now she was worried and search parties were sent out across the moors to see if he had perhaps fallen into a burn or a ditch somewhere. There was no sign of him. For three days his family and friends looked everywhere for Willie, but not a sight of him could be found. Sadly, they came to the conclusion that he had lost his way and wandered off towards the shore. It had happened often enough in the past that men with a bit of a glow on had ended up drowned in the wild seas that surround the Shetland Isles. Willie's wife was devastated and his children, a girl and a boy, were distraught. Everyone else felt that Willie and his fiddle would be sorely missed; he was a decent fiddler and had given his neighbours hours of pleasure. But life had to go on.

So time passed and even the grief of his immediate family began to ease a little. They came to the point where they could speak about him without somebody bursting into tears, though there was a heavy air of gloom over the household that wouldn't shift. The neighbours were sympathetic and thought that time would, as in all things, help to ease their sorrow.

A year passed and the house was decked out in black in honour of the lost husband and father. That night his wife and children went to bed with heavy hearts and tear-stained eyes.

In the morning, a year and a day from that fateful wedding, Willie's wife opened the door. There, stood in front of her, fiddle under his arm and a big smile on his lips, was Willie. She gave a great shriek and fainted dead away. The bairns came running with no hesitation to their father.

'Daddy, daddy,' they cried, 'where hae ye been all this time? Oh, daddy, it's grand to see you.'

Willie just smiled and lifted his wife into a chair.

'Ach weel, I cannae tell ye where I've been, but I'm glad tae be hame wi you all. Jean,' he said to the eldest, 'get your mother a drink of water.'

As Janet came round he fed her some water and gently stroked her hair, as he had always liked to do. Slowly she realised that this was no apparition; it really was Willie. Once she got over the shock, she was overjoyed. But that too didn't last.

'Willie Clarke, what dae you mean doin this to us? Where hae ye been all this time? It's been a year and a day since thon weddin,' she said. At that, she thought: a year and a day – just the length of time the old people and the old songs and stories said a fairy spell would last. A look of understanding came into her eyes.

'Weel, I cannae tell ye where I've been, Janet, but I havnae been off with another woman if that's what ye're thinkin,' he said, smiling. He realised by the dawning look in her eyes she had a pretty fair idea where he had been.

'Right then,' she replied, giving him a kiss, 'we'll say nae mair about it.'

That day there was a great party in the Clarke household and, as word spread round the area, friends and neighbours came flocking round to see the missing man who had come back. Many asked where he had been, usually with a fair idea of what the answer was, but all Willie would say, with a smile, was, 'My lips are sealed.' Of course with such a gathering in the house, Willie was called on to play the fiddle, and play he did. If he had been a good fiddler before, it was obvious he was a better one now, and there were a few knowing glances amongst some of the older people as the dancing started.

Not long after Willie returned from his year away, life began to take a turn for the better for him and his family. Whenever he went out in his boat he always brought home a good catch, even when others were coming home empty-handed. His crops were always healthy and bad weather that decimated other peoples' barley and oats in the run-up to harvest seemed to pass him by. He was in greater demand than ever as a fiddler for weddings and other rants and foys, as parties were called in Shetland back then. It was noted at such events that he also seemed to have a few new tunes that no one had ever heard before. They were strangely different to the normal music played by the Shetland fiddle fraternity and people loved dancing to them. So he was asked to play at even more events. His wife had three more bonnie babies one after the other – boy, girl, boy – and each one was as happy as the one before was healthy. People of course began to put two and two together and it was generally thought that there must be magic involved somewhere along the way. One night, around midnight, a passing neighbour saw Willie heading out from his croft, fiddle under his arm, after all the family were asleep, and disappearing in the direction of the Knowe. In truth, it was something he did a lot of the time, ever since he had come back from his long disappearance. There were also strange sounds sometimes heard late at night around the Clarke croft, and people began to make sure they avoided that part of the island after dark if they could. Still, Willie was a grand fiddler and the demand for his services was in no way weakened. In fact, he was going from strength to strength.

This went on for many years and his family grew up fit and well, his crops and fishing were always good and he began to be able to save some money. In short, he prospered. Many a time people tried to get Willie to say how he had come into such good luck but he would simply say, 'My lips are sealed,' and smile a wee, strange smile.

It was nearly twenty years later that Willie played at the wedding of his younger daughter. She had made a grand match with a lad from the other end of the island and all day Willie's elbow was jinking and diddling, if not with the bow then with a glass. By the time the bride and groom were convoyed off by the bridal party to their new home, the bride's father was as fou as he had ever been. After most of the company had gone home or off to bed, Willie was left having a last dram, or three, with a couple of his new son-in-law's relations. One of them, Norrie

Tamson, in his early twenties, was himself a fiddler and they had played together for much of the day.

'Ye're a fine fiddler, Norrie,' said Willie, slurring his words a little. 'Stick at it and you'll be somethin, mark my words.'

'Och, I dinnae think I'll ever get to be as good as you though, Mr Clarke,' said the youngster.

'Aye,' said his elder brother Jimmy, 'you're a wonderful fiddler right enough, Mr Clarke.'

'Och aye, that I am,' said Willie, 'and I have been this past twenty years. Let's have another drink.'

Another round of whisky was poured and Jimmy asked. 'What happened twenty years ago, exactly?'

Willie looked at him through drink-misted eyes, his vision beginning to blur as the latest whisky hit the back of his throat. 'What? Twenty years ago, what?' he stuttered.

'You were saying you've been a braw fiddler these past twenty years, Mr Clarke,' said Norrie, realising despite the drink he had consumed that he might at last get the full story of how Willie Clarke's luck had changed.

'Och, aye. Right,' said Willie. 'All right, I'll tell ye. Though,' and he put a finger to his lips, 'it's a secret so ye've tae tell naebody. Right?'

The two young lads, now all ears, nodded. And so Willie Clarke told them how he had gone to the Knowe that night twenty years ago and seen a great door through which light was streaming. He looked in and was spotted by a great black trowe.

'A fiddler,' he shouted, 'just what we need. Come in, come in. Our own fiddler has been put under a spell by some human witch and cannae come, so you can take his place.' Willie, fired up by the whisky and music of the earlier wedding, was delighted to oblige and played throughout the night. A few hours later, another trowe fiddler had turned up and they played on together. This was the first of the strange and beautiful tunes he had become known for – they truly were trowie music. Even after he had got home and realised the night had been a year and a day, he decided to keep in touch with the trowes as he loved their music so much. So for many years he had been going off and playing with trowe fiddlers at their rants and it was this relationship that had guaranteed his luck down all the years.

'So, what do you think of that then, lads,' he said as he finished. Just as he asked, he realised that his eyes were failing him. And suddenly he was sober. But his eyesight didn't improve.

From then on Willie's luck changed again. Within a week he was blind. Soon his crops began to fail and there was no way he could get himself back to the Knowe alone. He tried going back with his sons leading him, but any time he went nothing happened. Where before there had always been a trowie fiddler waiting when he arrived, now he could hear nothing but the wind blowing. Luckily his sons were still fit and well and working; otherwise it could have gone bad with him and his wife indeed. As it was, their house became full of horrible sounds and smells every night immediately after nightfall; within a month he was forced to abandon his croft and go to live with his son in Lerwick. The noises and smells from the house got even worse and soon the minister insisted that it be pulled down. Soon after that, Willie Clarke went off to join his ancestors. Since then no one has ever lived on the croft, which had for so long been the site of such beautiful music. Trowe music played by a human hand had been a wondrous thing indeed. The human hand had been good enough, but the human lips had not remained sealed as they should have been.

A Fiddler's Chase

Once, a long time ago in a village in Scotland, there was a local lad who had a bit of a name as a fiddler. His name was David and he was a shy young man who liked nothing better than going around playing music to people who were sick. The people of the village thought highly of him and it was commented that, after a visit or two, the sick generally seemed to recover. This was put down to the restorative power of music and to some extent to his sympathetic manner and consideration for the invalids. The truth was that he was a powerful magician! He had been raised by an uncle, who taught him to believe that the powers he had discovered in himself should only ever be used for good purposes; his love of playing the fiddle gave him a good cover for his activities. Well aware that there were others with similar powers who used them either for their personal gain or even to work evil, he had set himself clearly in a path of only doing good. He thought that he would never attempt to use his powers for his own good, but the best intentions can aye gang agley.

The villagers had no idea of his powers, though they all realised that there was something special about David, and many felt particularly kindly towards him. However, there was one person in the village who didn't see him in quite the same way. Her name was Sandra and she was a beautiful young woman, with gorgeous grey-green eyes, thick and lustrous fair hair, a beautiful sweet mouth and a full womanly figure. She was well aware of her good looks and the effect she had on men, and she enjoyed the flattery of their attention. At one time or another, all of the young men from her own and other nearby villages had attempted to woo her. However, she was a proud, impetuous and utterly selfish being. From her birth her mother had indulged her every whim and, as she grew older, she came to expect that she would always get her own way. This usually proved to be the case for she too was possessed of considerable magic powers. These she had in some way inherited from her grandmother, who had been burned as a witch many years before. Her mother had no such powers and doted on her daughter, never suspecting that the magic of her mother had skipped a generation and been reborn in her daughter. Sandra's beauty and haughty manner, though they turned the heads of the young men, were distrusted by many of the villagers. Some of them were pretty sure that she had inherited her grandmother's witching ways and, when things went wrong – crops failing or animals dying – there were some who could be heard muttering that she was behind it. They might think that she was responsible for such calamities, but they were frightened of her and none of them was prepared to confront her. Generally, the villagers went out of their way to avoid upsetting her and quite a few just tried to keep out of her way completely.

It was inevitable that the two magicians should become aware of each other, and each other's powers, but what was perhaps surprising was that David fell in love with the beautiful Sandra. He knew fine well that she was a real minx and dangerous to boot but he lost his heart to her totally. Despite his considerable powers, his shyness wasn't just a front, and he found it impossible to speak of his love directly.

Sandra, of course, understood that the young magician was in love with her but she had such a high opinion of herself that she thought no one good enough for her. She wasn't stupid and realised that if she were ever to find herself a partner it might be preferable to have someone who understood her powers. The alternative was to ensnare a normal human and, despite her pride and high opinion of herself, she realised that such an arrangement might soon bore her. However, she wasn't sure that she wanted anybody at all, so she simply decided to ignore her fellow magician. Then things changed.

One Sunday she was sitting in her house when she heard the sweet sound of David's fiddle playing a beautiful slow air below her window. Even without any magical powers he was a very fine fiddler indeed, and she sat enjoying his playing for about an hour. The music stopped; when she went to the window she saw that the young magician had gone. He hadn't stayed to say anything at all. Now Sandra, despite herself, was a bit flattered and even allowed herself to think kindly of David – for a moment or two. Then she decided he was being presumptuous and decided to go back to ignoring his actions. However, when the following Sunday he again began to play beneath her window, she took affront and decided to test the power of her suitor.

She summoned up her magical powers and changed herself into a rose, growing in the centre of her garden. Realising what was happening, her suitor followed her example and used his magic. He changed into a bee and began to buzz around the rose, pecking it with kisses. This was not what she had had in mind at all! So she decided to change herself into a queen bee. No sooner was this done than David turned into a hive enclosing her. Her temper now up, Sandra changed into a swallow and flew off into a tree, closely followed by David in the shape of a kestrel, hunting her down. So she became a lark and soared away up high into the clouds above. Not to be outdone, he became a great golden eagle and climbed up high to her. Straight to the earth she fell like a stone and changed into an eel, wriggling through the burn at the foot of her garden. Immediately, he became a great pike chasing the eel.

By now she was furious; whatever she changed herself into he seemed to be able to come up with a way to threaten to catch her. He might have had no words to say to her in human form but in the magic contest he was surely showing his mettle. Sandra was not impressed, though she was angry. Coming from the water, she changed herself into a stoat, ounce for ounce one of the fiercest animals on the planet. David was up to the test, though, and became an otter chasing the stoat. Next she changed herself into a mare standing on the side of a nearby hill and, to her surprise, David turned himself into a saddle clinging tightly to her back. She bucked and jumped and jumped and bucked but the saddle would not shift. She felt as if he were suffocating her in the clasp of his arms. In an instant she changed herself to a seed of corn lying on the floor of the chicken run back at her home. David turned himself into a proud big rooster and was just about to peck her up when again she shape-shifted and became a reed in pond. Imagine her distress when a shepherd pulled the reed for a pipe. As the shepherd put the reed to his lips she realised that it was him, David, yet again, kissing her as he played. So she became a boat, but felt him all around her as the ocean. Try as she might she could not get away. She became a mug in a nearby tavern and he returned to his human form and lifted the mug to his lips, kissing her yet again. Almost blind with rage by now, she thought she knew how to stop him touching her.

She became the griddle sitting over the fire in the tavern, but just as she completed the shift he turned himself into a great bannock, covering all of the griddle. Could she do nothing to escape, she roared silently to herself and took a real chance. She turned herself into a religious icon on the wall of a nearby church. David, though, had no fear of this shrine and came into the church as a deacon, walked up to the icon and began covering it with kisses. By now she was white with fury and determined to best him. So she let herself become infected with disease and lay in her bed at home. He, of course, came and began to play his fiddle, playing the very tunes that had helped so many invalids recover. But Sandra was made of stern stuff, and she used her powers to resist the healing process, and in her resistance, she died there on her bed. Being a talented magician, she knew she could return to life. But to thwart her ardent suitor she allowed herself to be buried in the kirkyard of the little church on whose wall she had briefly passed as an icon. That would teach him, she thought! But as she lay there she became aware that he had turned himself into the earth that enclosed her and once more it was as if she was clasped in his loving arms.

So her soul rose up, but there at the very gates of heaven itself she realised that David's power was such that he had turned himself into St Peter to welcome her into heaven. He had followed her even this far! Suddenly she began to understand that she had tested him to the limit and he had not been found wanting.

So, she concentrated all of the strength that remained within her and once more she was sitting in her room overlooking the garden of her mother's house. Within a split second David stood before her, fiddle in hand and a shy smile on his handsome features. She looked closely and realised what his shyness had caused her to miss. He was indeed a handsome man.

'Very well, then,' she said, trying to speak in a cold tone of voice, 'you are persistent. I'll give you that.'

He took her hand and raised it to his lips. Kissing her hand, he murmured, 'It is only that I love you above all else. Will you be mine?'

Sandra blushed from the roots of her hair to the soles of her feet. What was she feeling? Her emotions were all mixed up. True, he was persistent, but who did he think he was, asking for her hand? Yes, he was handsome, and charming and talented, but . . . but . . . Then all at once she realised that deep in her heart she loved this man who had chased her so avidly through all her shape-shifting and who had withstood her apparent indifference. And so she consented to become David's wife. Soon word went around the village that they were to be wed. Many people were hardly surprised that Sandra was not in fact dead; those that had murmured about her being a witch felt quite smug. The majority of the villagers were actually more taken aback at her acceptance of David, the shy fiddler. Some of them did put two and two together and realised that there was a lot more to the fiddler than met the eye. Sandra, of course, was considerably taken aback at how easily she was accepted back into village life. And she was disappointed that no one had seemed to miss her very much, not even her own mother.

So they were married and the villagers' fears of her began to weaken as time passed. For, listening every evening to the wonderful fiddling of her handsome young husband, and spending time with this pure-hearted soul, she herself began to mellow. Soon she was accompanying her husband on his visits to the sick and would sit by him as he played his healing music, and within just a few years they were considered to be as fine and happy a young couple as the village had ever seen.

A Price to Pay

Now, early in the eighteenth century in Fife there was a young man by the name of Davie Haxton who loved music, particularly the fiddle. Nothing would have pleased him more than to be able to play an instrument himself and give pleasure to others. However, no matter how hard he tried, he seemed to be utterly incapable of learning to play a single note. When his attempts at getting music from the fiddle resulted in nothing but horrible skraichs and squeaks he tried his hand at the trumpet. He had no better luck. When he tried the harp he failed there too. In fact every instrument he tried, even the Jew's Harp, proved to be beyond his abilities. His continuing failures drove him nearly demented. But Davie was a stubborn sort of creature and resolved that, come hell or high water, he would learn to play an instrument.

So he decided he would have to try magic. He waited till the morning of Halloween and, before dawn had streaked the sky, he crept out of the house that he shared with his parents and brothers and sisters. He had already picked his spot to make his attempt at magic. He had found a strong brier that was rooted in the ground at both ends, forming an arc just big enough for him to crawl under. So, just as dawn was rising he took off all of his clothes and, calling on the devil himself for the power of music, he crawled under the brier. Nine times he crawled on all fours under that brier and by the end he was shivering with cold and bleeding in several places, where thorns had ripped his flesh.

Standing up, he turned to where he had left his clothes and there, lying on top of his jacket, was a fiddle!

It was a strange old-fashioned looking thing with just one string and beside it was an equally hoary old bow. Without even putting on his clothes, he picked up the fiddle and the bow. Tucking the bow under his chin and laying the bow across the strings, he attempted to draw out a note. Instantly, it was as if he had been playing all his life. His fingers found a series of notes of their own volition and his right arm caressed the string with the bow. It was marvellous. A wonderful haunting tune, one he had never heard before, came out of the instrument. Never had he heard such a beautiful tune and he was playing it himself! His plan had worked and his request had been granted.

Quickly he dressed and ran home. His family were just sitting down to breakfast without him when he burst in and, without a word, played them the tune. They were astounded and asked him to play it again and again. He was happy to do so and soon all the neighbours heard of his new-found skill. The strange thing was he could only play the one tune. But it was a tune people could not get enough of. Every time they heard it, it was like the first time, and Davie soon became popular at dances and weddings all over the area. His tune wasn't suitable for dancing, but whenever there was call for a slow air Davie would be called for and he would play the tune, over and over again. Such was his popularity that he began to make some money; he began to play further and further from home as his fame spread. Davie found playing at fairs particularly rewarding; one day he went to Dunfermline, where there was to be a great fair and people from all over Scotland would be coming to buy and sell horses.

As usual, people loved to hear him play his tune, over and over again. Although he realised that he could only play because of magic, he cared little. He had always wanted to be a musician and now, with people applauding him and showering money on him, he was truly content. He felt as if he didn't have a care in the world. It was a fine autumn day and there were hundreds of people moving about the stalls that had been set up. There were several musicians, pipers and fiddlers, but none was doing as well as Davie. All day he had a good crowd around him and they were as generous as people always were when they heard him play his magic tune.

Now, in the crowd that day there was a Frenchman. He had come all the way from the French court to buy horses and, having found none that he thought were up to scratch, he was wandering around the fair when he heard the sound of Davie's fiddle. At once he was smitten with the sweet sounding tune and resolved there and then to ask Davie to come back with him to France. He knew the king loved music; bringing this remarkable musician back with him might make up for the fact that his trip to Scotland had been so unsuccessful up till then. So he hung around, entranced by the music, till Davie at last finished and put away the old one-string fiddle into the bag he carried it in.

At once the Frenchman approached him.

'Monsieur,' he said, 'perhaps I could have a word with you?'

Davie looked at this man with a foreign accent and noticed that he was very well dressed indeed. He must be a gentleman – maybe even a nobleman of some kind.

'Aye,' he replied, 'whit can I do for ye?'

'I would like for you to come to France with me,' said the Frenchman, with a smile.

'France!' Davie said with a start. 'That's an affy long way away from here.'

'Yes, it is,' said the nobleman, 'but I would like you to come and play at the French court for our king. He is very fond of music and I have never heard anyone play like you do. I am certain my king will reward you very well once he has heard you playing your old fiddle.'

Now, Davie had been thinking that he was doing very well up till then. But to be asked to go and play for royalty – well, that

115

was beyond his wildest dreams. He had no hesitation in agreeing at once and, without even sending word back to his family, he left for France the very next day with his new companion. With the success of his playing he had become very self-confident; the idea of heading off to a foreign country where he knew no one and couldn't even speak the language didn't bother him at all. In fact, he was looking forward to it.

A few days later the pair of them arrived in Paris. Davie was set up in a fancy apartment while the nobleman went off to arrange matters. The fiddler was waited on hand and foot, with the very best of food and drink served to him by a couple of very bonny young lasses. Now, Davie had no French at that point but he wasn't going to let that stop him taking full advantage of his situation. A day or so later his new friend arrived and took him off to a tailor to be kitted out in the latest fashion at the court. Things were just getting better and better for him!

Once he was suitably dressed in velvet and lace, his companion brought round a carriage and then the pair of them headed off to the palace of Versailles, where the French king held his court.

That evening, the French nobleman brought Davie to the court and had him play for the king. Just like everyone else who had ever heard him play, the king was smitten with love for Davie's tune. He could not hear it often enough and so it became a nightly occasion whenever the king was at Versailles – he had to hear Davie play his tune at least once. Sometimes, when he went off hunting to other parts of France or to have meetings with other great men, he would take Davie along. And everywhere Davie went people simply adored his music. This was more than he had ever hoped for and soon he was rich and admired throughout France. Anything he wanted, he got. In fact, he was living the life of a French aristocrat, a long way from the humble village life he had been born into on the banks of the Tay.

Time and again other musicians asked to play his one-string fiddle, and time and again they failed. No one seemed to be able to get more than an odd note here and there from it. Other musicians, fiddlers, trumpeters and harpers all tried to replicate Davie's tune but no one could ever manage it. Even the very best of the musicians at the French court, who could catch most of Davie's melody, were incapable of making it sound like Davie. A few of them muttered that he was in league with the devil, but this mattered little to the king who, as time went on, became even fonder of the tune, and its player. So Davie became a real favourite at the court and, no matter what might be said behind his back, he had the king's support so could do virtually what he wanted, as long as he was there to play, every evening. It was a life of nothing but luxury and Davie loved every minute of it.

Things carried on like this for many years and both Davie and the king were beginning to move into middle age. The fiddler had by now learned to speak French fluently, though he never lost his accent. He was still occasionally gently mocked by some of the younger ladies of the court, but all in good fun, for no one wanted to offend 'le Violer Ecossais', the king's favourite. Then, one dark winter's night at about three in the morning, the whole court of Versailles was awakened by a great noise. It was a simple two-note musical phrase but it rang out like a thunderclap. It was so loud peoples' ears were ringing with it; it took a few minutes for them to come completely to their senses. Guards were sent to search the entire palace complex to see if they could find out the source of this awesome sound. When they knocked on Davie's door the guards got no answer. Bursting in, they found him lying in his bed with a look of abject horror on his face. The Scottish fiddler was dead. And there, on the floor beside his bed, were the shattered remains of an old one-string fiddle and a bow. It was said all over the court that the whisperers had been right and Davie had been in league with the devil. He had had a good run for his money, but in the end he had to pay the price for his magic music!

Name that Tune

Some stories are quite specifically associated with the composing and naming of certain tunes – tunes that are very much still in the traditional fiddle repertoire today.

The Reel o Tulloch

There are several versions of how this famous tune came into being, some claiming a piping origin and others saying it was originally played on the fiddle. The fiddle version is that the tune originated in Tulloch in Strathspey, an area famed for its fiddlers for a long time. It seems that, some time early in the eighteenth century, the countryside was hit with a terrible winter. Many of the lochs and even some of the rivers were frozen and the land was covered with ice and snow. Blizzards were frequent and the trees sparkled with frozen snow. When the sky was clear the country was beautiful, but dangerous. However, the local people tried their very best to get on with life as usual. One Sunday most of the congregation turned up at the Tulloch church, despite a blizzard blowing for most of the morning. Many of the congregation had travelled several miles in dreadful conditions, but when they got there they found no minister. Some said he had been caught up in the storm while coming back from visiting one of his more distant parishioners the previous day; others maintained that he had looked out of his window that morning from the manse at Milton of Tulloch, a few miles away, and concluded that none of his congregation were likely to try and brave that kind of weather to get to Sunday service. So he had poured himself a dram of whisky and hunkered down by his own fire for the day.

The service was supposed to start at eleven in the morning and by half past the hour people were beginning to get a bit impatient. There they sat, well wrapped up in plaids and blankets; but after even a short time in that biting cold they began to lose feeling in their feet and hands. Soon the discreet rubbing of hands and genteel tapping of feet became something more. Most of the congregation that day were on the young side; many of the older people had stayed at home because of the vicious weather and the dangerous conditions underfoot. When another quarter of an hour had passed, the stamping of feet and flapping of hands was universal. It was bitterly cold. One thing soon led to another. One or two of the children began to run around the kirk – something that would normally have brought a hard skelp on the ear, or somewhere even more tender. More and more people began to move about; those who remained sitting were soon stamping their feet and clapping their hands. Taking their lead from the children running around and enjoying themselves in being allowed to play in the church, the grown-ups too decided to have some fun.

One of the elders, a man called Davidson, suggested that the usual collection be taken while they were waiting for the minister to arrive.

'That's a good idea,' said local fiddler David Broun, 'but if he doesnae come soon we mebbe could get something to warm us up wi the money.'

There were mutterings of agreement and the normally serious Davidson realised that the idea of a wee dram on such a freezing cold day was one that had an appeal to many of the congregation, himself included. Normally, he would haven't given any consideration to what Broun said. It was well known he was one of the tinker Brouns, who had a bit of a reputation for mischief in

119

the area, but David himself led a steady life and, like many of his family, was a fair hand with the fiddle. After all, this was an unusual situation: the weather was so cold it was dangerous; there was no sign of the minister, so something had to be done. In those days, before the invention of central heating, churches were notoriously cold places even at the very best of times.

So when after another ten minutes or so the minister still hadn't turned up, a couple of young men were sent off to buy some whisky with the elder's blessing. The fact that they were lads who were in the business of making peatreek was considered handy. They were back within minutes; obviously they had a nearby cache of illicit whisky, something Elder Davidson was probably aware of. Like many another respectable member of the community he was well aware of the medicinal advantages of whisky, as well as its convivial effects.

A quaich, the traditional small communal drinking vessel of the Scots, appeared from somewhere (probably the peatreekers kept one handy at all times) and was filled with whisky. It was passed around the entire congregation with lots of lip-smacking and sighs of contentment, being refilled after every three or four drinks. However, even if it was making everyone feel a bit better it did not affect the coldness in the air. People were still moving around, stamping their feet and flapping their arms to try and keep warm, though they were all well wrapped up in good thick woollen clothes. As the quaich went round a second time – well, the minister still hadn't shown up – a friend of David Broun piped up. 'Davie, lad, if you went and got your fiddle we could have a wee bit dance – it would keep us warm till the minister gets here.'

A muttered aside was heard: 'If he ivver does.'

There were nods of agreement and a few people spoke up: 'Good idea,' 'Aye, get yer fiddle, Davie.'

So Broun went off through the snow to fetch his fiddle. It didn't take him long; he lived close by. As soon as he got back, he struck up a tune and the congregation started to dance.

Between dances the quaich went round and, within the hour, a full-scale houlie was underway. Fired up by the occasion, and maybe just a little by the whisky, Broun launched into a new tune extempore. It worked out right away and to general shouts of encouragement from the crowd he played it again and again. And so the 'Reel o Tulloch' came into being. When all were tired of the dancing, a local shoemaker entered the pulpit and, inspired no doubt by the drink, gave a sermon that many local people swore was as good as any ever given by the minister. The evening ended with a 'gude and godly ballad', sung by the village blacksmith. For many years the locals spoke fondly of the day at the kirk when the 'Reel o Tulloch' was composed.

The Pict's Song

Until only a couple of centuries ago most people grew their own food. There were no shops or supermarkets and very little money, even if there had been places to buy food. Much of the trade that did go on was by the exchange of goods, or barter; even the rich folk in their big houses grew much of their own food, or rather had it grown for them in their extensive gardens. In general, people would have to take the crops they had grown themselves to local mills to be ground into flour, to make bread or bannocks. In those old days the diet of the people revolved to a considerable extent round barley and oats, with a few root vegetables and some meat and dairy products. Every area had its own mill, often owned by the landlord, and everybody had their turn to grind their corn. There was, of course, a charge for this and in many areas landlords made sure that leases declared that their tenants had to use their mills. The miller was thus a central figure in most communities and the mill itself was an essential community resource, and generally a profitable one. In some cases, the mills were operated directly by the smallholders or crofters themselves, and their rent would include a charge for the privilege. Rents were generally paid in kind, with food or other produce of the crofts.

On the eastern side of the Shetland island of Fetlar there was a mill known as Fir Vaa – a water mill. One night, Gilbert Lawrenson, who lived nearby, took his corn to the mill to grind it. He carried the great, heavy sack on his back and was relieved to get to the mill. He reckoned he could get some sleep while his corn was being ground. Emptying the corn into the hopper, he set the mill in motion and went off for a rest. Just beside the mill there was a wee house, little more than a shed really, where people could wait while the corn was ground. It was a pretty basic building, four walls and a roof, no fireplace and just a pile of straw to sit on. Still, it provided shelter from the wind, which, as any Shetlander will tell you, can get pretty wild on the islands.

This was at the time when snuff was very popular and, once Gilbert had sat himself down, he took some snuff and snuggled down into the straw. He wasn't quite asleep, just nodding away at the edge of sleep in a state a bit like day-dreaming. At first he thought he was dreaming when he began to hear music coming from outside by the mill. The music got a bit louder; suddenly Gilbert was fully awake. He knew, somehow, what was happening. Now, at this time, the Picts, the wee dark folk, were still about on the islands and they had a habit of stealing people's boats whenever they needed to journey between the islands. Fir Vaa was right down near the shore and Gilbert suspected that the peerie, or little fowk, as they were called locally, were coming in to land in a boat they had stolen. The Picts would take a boat and just leave it wherever it suited them; many a boat had been taken by them and left to drift off to sea. They were believed to have been forced into hiding by the coming of the big people, the current Shetlanders, and generally only came out at night. Now, the people needed their boats to catch fish to eat, and maybe sometimes, if they were lucky, to sell to passing ships. The Picts' stealing of the boats was considered a real plague among the islanders. Gilbert was fully awake now and heard the Picts land the boat on the beach. The music got even louder; it sounded as if they were coming straight towards the wee house by the mill! Gilbert didn't know what to do, so he buried himself as deep as he could in the pile of straw he had been lying on, and pretended to be asleep.

In came the Picts and saw him lying there. Some of them wanted to play tricks on him, but one of them just said, 'Ach, let him be. I've seen this one about the place; he's all right. Let him sleep.' All this time the music carried on and Gilbert opened his eyes – just a wee crack – to see what was going on.

'Come on, let's have another tune now, boy,' said one of the wee dark men, just out of Gilbert's sight. Slowly, so as not to give the game away, he moved as if in his sleep till he could see the musician. It was a tiny wee dark man with a porsh – an ancient one-stringed fiddle the Picts liked to play – and the wee fellow certainly could play it. As he played a lively, spirited tune with great gusto all the other Picts started to dance. Round and round they went as the musician played like the devil himself. They were all caught up in the music and paid no attention to Gilbert lying there in the straw. On and on the music went, right through the night and on to the morning. Gilbert felt as if he was caught in a dream, listening to the tune as it was repeated time and again through the hours of darkness.

Then, as the sun came up, the music came to an abrupt end. The Picts stopped their dancing and, without a word, they all went out of the wee house. Gilbert lay still till he heard their footsteps fade as they headed into the hinterland of the island, where they were thought to live in underground houses like their ancestors of old. It was widely believed that the Picts had considerable magic powers and people were keen to avoid them if at all possible.

Only when he was sure that the Picts were well away did Gilbert think to move. He quickly went to the mill to get his flour. He filled his sack and, as he did so, he kept humming the tune the wee Pict had been playing most of the night on his porsh. Once he had his flour, he hoisted the big sack on his back again and set off home, all the time humming and whistling the Pictish tune. He thought he would come back and have a look at the boat the Picts had landed in later on. Now, Gilbert had a pretty good ear for a tune but he was not much use on the fiddle. His son, though, wee Gibbie, was turning out to be a very fine fiddler indeed. So, as soon as he got home, without explaining where he had been all night to his stern-faced wife, Gilbert told his son to fetch his fiddle and whistled the tune to him. Once, twice and then a third time he whistled the tune and wee Gibbie, caught up in his father's excitement, dashed it off on the fiddle, almost note perfect. A few wee changes were all that was necessary and the boy had the tune. Only then did Gilbert turn to his wife. 'I was caught up in the wee hoose at the mill, lass. In came a bunch o Picts and they played their fiddle and danced all night. That's the tune they were playin that wee Gibbie has just learned.' And he stood there smiling.

His wife was relieved at the news, even if she was a bit frightened he had been all night in the same house as a bunch of Picts. For she knew well, as did everyone, that they could be right bad and spiteful wee creatures. But her man was safe, so it was all right, and she had to admit that the tune was a fine one. Gilbert himself was pleased that he had got one over on the Picts by stealing one of their tunes, and when word got round everybody wanted to hear wee Gibbie play it.

And that is how the tune they call 'Winyadepla' became part of the Shetland repertoire. The name was taken from the wee lochan above the Lawrensons' croft, though wee Gibbie always called it 'Old Gibbie's Tune', in honour of his father.

Jenny Dang the Weaver!

Even back in the eighteenth century there were some in the ministry who liked a good tune. Although some sectors of Scottish Presbyterianism retained the Reformation distrust of any form of human enjoyment, some ministers were just like their parishioners. Some even learned to play the fiddle themselves. One of these was the Reverend Alex Garden, who was born in 1700 and became minister at Birse in Aberdeenshire when he was twenty-six, remaining there till his death in 1777. Apart from his skill with the bow, the Reverend Garden was also a composer and a poet and possessed of a ready wit. A new odd-job man, Tam Lewis, had been appointed at the manse to help around the house and with the running of the glebe, that stretch of land that was given every minister to help him grow his own food. The ministers' stipends, or salaries, were no more generous then than they are now (according to what the few ministers I have met have told me!). Tam had been a hand-loom weaver, well set up in his cottage with his loom, a wife and a growing family. Sadly, he had fallen on hard times through helping members of his immediate family and had ended up in debt. This had forced him to sell his loom and he had become a jack of all trades at the manse, a position he resented. He felt he had come down in the world a fair way and, though he had to work to feed and house his family, he was not exactly a willing worker all the time.

Now, the minister liked nothing better of an evening than to sit playing his treasured Cremona violin, trying out new compositions or old favourites. He would spend many hours in his study, playing away for no one's amusement but his own. Never on a Sunday though! One evening he was at his favourite pastime while waiting to be called for dinner, when he heard a stramash in the manse kitchen. There was an awful clattering and yelling and the minister was sure he even heard a few expletives. Putting down his violin, he headed towards the kitchen, not knowing what to expect. There in the centre of the kitchen was his wife, Mysie, walloping Tam the odd-job man over the shoulders and head with the beetle, the wooden mallet with which she was wont to mash the potatoes and neeps (turnips) her husband enjoyed so much with his dinner.

'What is going on here?' demanded the minister, as Tam fell to the floor below the fierce onslaught of Mrs Garden.

'This cheeky creature here,' his wife stuttered, 'this ingrate, this, this, this impertinent . . .'

'Calm down, Mysie,' said the minister, moving between his irate wife and man cowering on the floor. 'Just tell me what happened.'

'What happened? What happened?' sputtered Mysie, sounding quite hysterical.

'Now, calm yourself, woman,' the minister said sternly. 'Just sit yourself down on this chair.' He pushed her onto a chair, none too gently. 'Just you sit there and I'll get you a glass of water.'

Before getting her a glass of water, though, he turned and helped Tam up off the floor and ushered him gently out of the kitchen. Pouring the glass of water for his wife, he handed it to her and pulled up a chair to sit facing opposite her.

'Now, my love, just tell me what happened,' he said gently.

Mysie gulped a drink of water and took a deep breath.

'Well, I've never . . . no. Wait a minute.' She took another deep breath and proceeded to tell the minister that she had told Tam – it was more asking really, she said – to clean the reverend's boots. Tam had bridled at the suggestion and said he hadn't been hired as a skivvy, but as an odd-job man. He clearly felt this was a task beneath him and Mysie had got so angry that she had walloped him with the beetle, which she had been using to mash the tatties. As she was telling the tale the minister's eyes began to glow and he was soon having difficulty in suppressing a laugh. In those far-off days physical abuse was rarely thought of as anything to worry about much and, having got over the shock of seeing his prim and proper wee wife belabouring the substantial odd-job man, the minister was beginning to see the funny side of the situation.

Barely keeping a straight face, he said, 'Well, just keep calm. I'm sure everything will work itself out. I'll have a word with Tam after we have eaten. Just you get back to the dinner and I'll go into my study till we're ready to eat.'

At that he got up and went back to his study, a big grin all over his face. In fact, he was so taken with what he had seen that he picked up his violin, laid the bow across the strings and, in less than five minutes, had added a new tune to our national repertoire of fiddle tunes. And what could he call it but 'Jenny Dang the Weaver'!

A Fiddler Looks Back

Auld Tam lived in the hills near Peebles. All his life he had been an active man, working mainly as a shepherd, but turning his hand to various other jobs in the course of a long life. He had even played the fiddle a bit and accompanied some well-known musicians of his time. Now, in the latter half of the nineteenth century, he was well into his eighties and he liked little more than to sit at the door of his cottage when the weather permitted. During the long winter nights was often to be found seated by the fire in the tavern a mile from his home. Here, over a glass of porter, his fiddle on the table before him, he would reminisce about the old days, sometimes with men of his own generation and sometimes with younger men and lads who liked to hear him talk of the old days.

He would tell them of men like Jamie Dyer, a wandering fiddler and a famous man in the Borders in the 1840s. The old man took a sip from his glass and started . . .

I mind Jamie Dyer at a dance we had one time in late November in Langholm, away back in 1841. Now, Jamie was a bit o a lad, a fine enough fiddler but a laddie wi a sharp eye for the siller. His regular way o startin things was tae say something like, 'Welcome, awbody, tae the dance here in Langholm. It's a place dear tae ma heart as I was married twenty year ago on Langholm Hiring Day.' This was the day when the fairmers would take on the fowk they needit for the next year's work on their farms. Nou, I hae nae idea when Jamie was actually married, for he would say exactly the same thing in Kelso, or Gala or even doun in Peebles. Ye see, it was part o his philosophy o aye giving the customers what they wanted. He told me it helped tae put the customers at their ease an that tended to make them enjoy the entertainment better. He could explain awa just about anythin, could Jamie.

That night the dance was the usual kind o thing. He'd hired the hall himself, brought along me and Old Wattie Tamson on the bass fiddle, hired a couple o young lads to look after the door, and another pair o aulder fellows to be on hand to keep order. Ye were charged at the door, usually a penny or so, and there was aye young lads trying to get in for free. Even if they had the money they'd try it on, but I shouldna say anything for I did it myself when I was just a laddie. But Jamie was aye strict aboot that kind o thing. 'I'll hae nae tricky youngsters takkin siller fae ma pooch,' he'd say, for, like I said, he was pretty much aware o the value o the coinage. So we were all set that night in Langholm. We'd hired a barn fae a fairmer just outside the toun and Jamie had spent the day going round the shops and telling people there was a dance on.

He'd got somebody to put up a few posters in the inns and the Post Office as well, and he was hopin for a good turn-out once the word had got around. People were lookin forward to haein a good dance and in the mood for a bit o fun. We started at ten o'clock at night and, as usual, a few of the young lads were a bit fou. We all worked gey hard in those days and if you got a chance to have some fun there was nae holdin back. Nou, the lads Jamie had hired tae keep an eye on things and tae make sure things didnae get out o hand were Willie Kemp an Johnny Braid, big powerful men in their thirties, but by the time we were off an playin they were gettin a bit fou themselves, sittin off in a corner near the door. We were on a stage made o hay bales and doun the left-hand side o the hall was a table where people could put the food they had brought wi them. The dance was due tae gang on to four in the morning, so you would need a bite to eat. People kept their drink by them, though – quarts o beer and porter, or bottles o whisky, most of it made up in the hills. You wouldnae be sae daft as to leave your drink alone; when people got up to dance it was some other body's job to watch their drink didnae get stolen. The worst for that was the youngsters though, laddies about twelve and thirteen, but you aye find somebody that takes pleasure in helpin themselves tae other's belongins, particularly drink I would say.

Well, we were due to stop for a wee break, and tak a glass or two ourselves at about midnight. I mind looking out over the room an thinkin it was grand. We were well rehearsed and had been playin together for quite a whilie, so the music was fine. But the dancin, nou that was something else again. Jamie might cry for a Strathspey, or a reel or even a polka, but there was always them that wanted to tak their own road. That night, lookin out fae the stage, I saw whit ye might call a range o dancing styles – at one end o the hall there was Bob McLehose doin something like a Highland Fling and at the other end auld Geordie Keiller, dancing like he aye did. It didnae matter tae Geordie whit time the tune was in, he went at his ain pace, shufflin an swayin tae some kind o rhythm that only he could hear. An then there was the lad they called the Big Plooman, Archie Gilfeather; he was six and a half feet tall and could lift a man single-handedly in the end o a shovel. Well, I cannae be sure exactly what he was doin, but it was some kind o double shuffle. Dancin with him, or in front of him anyway, was wee Jessie Gilchrist, a red-headed, sparky thing as nimble and trig in her feet as a deer.

Now, they say opposites attract, an maybe there's somethin to it. For there was Jessie, five feet nothin in her stocking soles, all dressed up in her finest dancin gear, wi Archie Gilfeather, the size o a barn himself an lookin like he could pick her up an put her in his pocket. As he was doin his double shuffle she was leapin an prancin on her toes, but all the time their eyes were fixed on each other. I could see there was a spark there. Jessie was a bonnie wee thing, just seventeen an shapely with it, an she had caught the eye o quite a few lads. But Archie, well, he was twenty-six an had never had a lot o luck wi the lasses before then. He was a canny lad an worked hard an could turn his hand to a lot o things that aye surprised people. He could fix watches and make horn spoons and fishin rods and all kinds o things. Those giant hands o his were capable o the maist delicate work an I suspect that Jessie somehow saw through the great bigness o the man to the delicacy beneath. Anyway, they were clearly fascinated by each other.

Now, as I said, Jessie had her admirers and a couple o the local lads had been competin tae win her hand for a half a year or more. They saw what was happenin. They were whisperin away to each other just as we stopped for the break. Jessie and the Big Plooman walked over to the table for a bite to eat and the pair o lads came over towards them. I was watchin an thinkin maybe somethin was about to happen. I looked around for Willie and Johhny to tip them the wink, but I couldnae see them in the corner. There were too many people movin towards the tables.

'Quick,' I said to Jamie, 'you'd better fetch Kemp and Braid; I think there's goin to be a bit o bother.'

I said this just as Jamie was lifting a glass to his lips; he paused and followed my gaze.

'Ach, dinnae you worry,' he replied, drinkin off the whisky. 'Those two lads cannae hurt Archie.'

Dyer clearly wasn't worried, so I went along wi him and we started up again. There was a brief kerfuffle when the two lads went at the Big Plooman, but the upshot was that he went by the front o the stage, draggin them by their collars. Both o them were knocked cold.

'Play on, play on, lads,' cried Jamie Dyer, so we did. It was aye the best policy to keep playin if there was any bother on the dance floor. If ye stopped it would just hae encouraged mair lads tae get involved – fightin was nae considered tae be that bad a thing in those days, an lots o the younger lads didnae think they had had a good nicht oot if they hadnae had a bit o a fight. But I reckon the twa lads that had a go at Archie wouldnae hae been so keen at the fightin after thon nicht. I noticed a wee while later, when they passed right in front o the stage, that wee Jessie was looking at Archie wi a right soft look. It came as nae surprise when their banns were cried a few weeks later. It ended up bein a braw dance an Jamie Dyer went hame in the mornin wi a big smile on his face. It had been a grand night; lots o fowk told Jamie how much they had enjoyed theirsels; the band were aw happy. But what pleased him most of aw was the money in his pocket!

The old fiddler took a sip from the glass in front of him, picked up his fiddle and played the company a fine old Strathspey before telling another story of Jamie Dyer:

Now Jamie, like most fiddlers, found it hard to resist the offer of a drink from a grateful audience. One time he ran into the local minister and the doctor late of a bright summer's evening. It was about midsummer, with a glorious clear sky. The minister and the doctor had been out seeing to a parishioner who wasn't expected to live much longer and were heading back home on horseback when they came across Jamie, who was unco' fou and had fallen in a ditch. He had been playing at a wedding a few miles away the day before and had met up with a group of the wedding guests around midday. Their generosity to the fiddler was such that his journey home was a complicated affair. He had ended up here on the moors, sprawling half in the ditch, and his case had fallen into the water at the foot of the ditch. That was bad enough, but, much worse than that, his fiddle had fallen out of its case. He'd only had the wooden case a few weeks; up till then he'd always carried his fiddle in a green velvet bag, like so many of the fiddlers in those days. Anyway, he was scrabbling about in the ditch looking for it when along comes the minister and the doctor on horseback. They pulled up and looked down at this drunk man guddling about in the ditch. And the minister turns to the doctor and says, 'Tut, Tut, a bad case indeed.'

'Tosh,' says the fiddler, over his shoulder, 'I widnae care tuppence about the case if I could only lay my hands on the fiddle.'

A Touchy Fiddler

Although the widespread popularity of the fiddle in the eighteenth and nineteenth centuries meant that there was always at least handful of truly inspired players in the country at any one time, there were always a few whose sheer lack of musical ability reminded people of the old cliché about fiddles – the tail of a horse being dragged over the guts of a cat. There were fiddlers who travelled the country picking up a few pennies wherever they could, and there were those whose use of the fiddle was no more than a handy cover for what was in truth begging. Some of these latter, no doubt, were forced into such activity by being incapable of doing anything else, through illness or plain lack of other opportunities. Mind you, there have always been those who, as the saying has it, 'werenae as daft as they put on'. At the time of the devastating Moray Floods of 1829 there was a street musician working the streets of Elgin called simply the Garb. As to what this nickname meant, we have no real idea. One day, a man from Tomintoul, high up in the hills, came down on a visit to Elgin.

He was wearing traditional Highland dress, with bonnet, kilt, sporran, sgian dubh and all. The Garb was much taken with his appearance when they met in the street.

The Highlander was with an old friend of his who lived in the town and was introduced to the scruffily-dressed creature with his old battered fiddle stuck under his arm. Following the actions of his friend, the Highlander handed over a halfpenny to the Garb before he had played a note.

'And how are we doing today, Garb?' asked the man from Elgin.

'Och, no bad, no bad, about the same as always. I make about twopence or threepence halfpenny most days, you know. It isn't a lot but it keeps me going. Would you like a wee tune now?' he asked, raising the decrepit fiddle to his chin and raising a bow that had very few horsehairs left on it. The Highlander, though no great expert, could see that the bow, like the fiddle, was well past its best.

'Well, that would be just fine,' said the Highlander, to the obvious horror of his friend. He realised what was going on and was having a bit of joke.

'Right then, I'll play you "The Haughs o Cromdale",' said the Garb. At that he struck a pose and launched into a rendition of something that might have been a tune, but then again might not have been. It was, in short, awful, and the Elgin man glared at his friend, who was clearly having trouble stopping himself from bursting into laughter. When the rendition was over, the musician looking expectantly at the man in Highland dress. His friend jumped in quickly.

'Right, Garb,' he said, 'for another penny, how about playing us "I Lost my Love and Care na"?' This was a popular tune of the time and the Highlander looked with some bemusement at his friend. Surely he wasn't seriously asking for yet more aural discomfort? His friend knew what he was doing, though, and the Garb took on a look of great solemnity, tucked his fiddle under his arm and spoke out clearly.

'Na, na, I'll never play thon tune again. Don't you know that I was deserted by my own sweetheart – and after our banns of marriage were published. She deserted me for another an I'll never play that tune again as lang as I live.'

With that, he turned on his heel and stomped off down the street, much to the relief of the Elgin man.

Turning to his friend with a look of reproach, he said, 'It's the only way to shut him up. You would have had him play on, wouldn't you, you daft bugger?'

'It would have been worth it just to watch your fizzog,' the Highlander laughingly replied. 'But tell me, how does he manage to make a regular income? He is truly the worst fiddler I have ever heard. The man has no ear for music at all.'

'Ach, we're not all daft in Elgin, you know. As the Garb tells it, there are five people in this town, all living along the High Street, who have no ear for music at all. Each of them pays him a halfpenny a day to pass their door without playing a note. They are spread out along the street, so we don't have to hear him play that much at all. He hasn't noticed yet that it isn't always exactly the same five people.'

Turning to look after the fiddler, the Highlander saw him turn up a side street; the sound of him sawing away at the fiddle came back to them. There was the Garb, walking along in the gutter, as always dragging horrible notes from his aged instrument but all with the air of utmost solemnity, a look he had seen good fiddlers adopt, and sure in himself that he was a musician of some standing. For, after all, he had a regular income from his playing, didn't he?

Jamie McQueen

As the eighteenth century unfolded, society underwent great changes. With the advance of industrialisation, cities expanded rapidly to accommodate the people coming in to work in the new factories. The increasing mechanisation of farming also meant that the old days, when there was a constant need for hundreds of pairs of hands to work the land, began to pass away. The people were forced to go and live in the cities or, as so many Scots have done, to emigrate to distant parts of the world. The old way of life of the farmtouns and small villages disappeared as farms got bigger. Increasingly, the country was covered with railway lines, drastically cutting down the time needed to travel between one place and another. People's horizons were expanding and many of the old trades such as the travelling pedlars and chapmen began to disappear. With the change in population, musicians too felt the change. No more could they be guaranteed a living travelling from farmtoun to farmtoun and village to village. People had not lost their love of music, however, and those who could move with the times did.

One of these was Jamie McQueen, a gifted fiddle player, who lived in Forres. Every morning at seven o'clock Jamie arose in the home he shared with his brother and got ready for his day's darg (shift). He would wash, eat breakfast made by his brother, then carefully put on full Highland regalia: kilt and sporran, stockings and brogues, a sgian dubh in the top of the right stocking, a frilled shirt and tweed jacket, a belt and full set of dirks, all topped off with a fine Glengarry bonnet. Then he would take down his fiddle case and check his fiddle and bow were in good working order. Snapping shut the case, he would head out to his place of work.

Every morning Jamie boarded the Aberdeen train. In those days the trains stopped at stations every few miles and, every time it stopped, Jamie would step out on to the platform and play a tune. Just as the train left he would get back in and would be rewarded by the passengers, many of whom would ask him to play their own favourite as the train sped on. At the next station, or the one after that if he found a receptive audience, he would again step out of the train and announce his presence to the travellers on the train. In this way he made a fair living and, as the summer came on and visitors began to come up to Morayshire to take the air, his takings would increase.

He would go as far as Aberdeen, have himself a bite to eat, and repeat the performance all the way back to Forres. By the time he was back he would have put in a hard day's work. He was always glad to get home, where his faithful brother would have a hot meal waiting. The times were changing and, as he himself said, we have to change with them.

A conscientious and committed musician, Jamie was also a bit of a poet. He was extremely proud to receive an acknowledgement from Queen Victoria herself when he sent her a copy of his published works. He hoped for many years that the queen might get to hear him on the journey between Forres and Aberdeen, but in this he was disappointed.

Fiddlers' Humour

G iven the social situations in which fiddlers have to work, it is hardly surprising that humour is a basic component in many of our stories. Those in this section are, with the exception of the joke at Dancey Mackenzie's expense in 'An Unusual Form of Dance', based on the sense of humour of fiddlers themselves.

A Fiddler's Joke

John Davidson was having an all-male soiree in his house on the island of Bute. Like many other successful men in his home city, he had built a home on the popular island in the Clyde, to which he and his family could escape from the crowded streets and the pollution of the industrial process that were giving Glasgow its wealth. The great ironworks, the ship-building and a hundred other industries were rapidly developing the city on the Clyde into the second city of the British empire after London. With the expansion of the empire all over the globe, there was an almost incessant demand for shipping; the shipyards along the Clyde were working flat out, turning out the very best vessels to be found anywhere. Bute had become a fashionable spot for those with the means to build houses there and regular ferries over the Clyde meant it was easy to get to after a short rail journey from Glasgow itself.

Now, Davidson had decided he wanted some music at his soiree and so he asked around locally for who was available. He ended up hiring a blind fiddler called Derek Barr who lived at Port Bannatyne, just up the road from Davidson's house overlooking the Clyde estuary at Rothesay. The very best of food and drink were laid on for the evening and the guests all arrived. Within a few minutes of the entertainment beginning, the atmosphere was electric. Barr was known as a fine fiddler, but this night his playing was absolutely first class. At the very first tune feet were tapping; after a couple of reels several of the men were up on their feet dancing. Truth to tell, several of them were fed up being taken to concerts of classical music by their wives – something that the wives considered was a natural adjunct to their 'place' in society – and the opportunity to revel in the traditional Scottish music so many of them had loved since childhood was one to be enjoyed. A passer-by looking in would have thought they were either all drunk or quite daft. There was hooching and clapping and the drink began to flow quite freely. It was truly a case of the old saying:

He made them dance who never danced before,
And those who always danced
To dance still more and more.

It was one of those nights when things went perfectly and Barr himself, by this time in his early sixties, was as excited as his audience. He knew fine well that he was playing at his very best and was having the time of his life. At last, he took a break to allow the dancers to catch their breath and take a sip or two of the very fine wine provided by their host. The host himself, Mr Davidson, was beside himself with pleasure. His party was going great guns and his plans could hardly have come to a better completion. As Barr took a breather and a wee thochtie of whisky specially provided for him, Davidson almost skipped across the room to congratulate him. He bent down and gave the blind fiddler a hug, nearly causing him to spill his drink. Then he stood back beaming. 'My dear wee man, you play brilliantly. But tell me, do you play by ear or what?'

The fiddler gave a wee smile. 'Year?' he queried, 'Och, I think that would gie ye a bit of a bellyfu o me. Nah, nah, sir, I generally jist play by the nicht.'

And Another

Ministers in Scotland have often had a bit of a bad press over the past few decades. The memories of how they used to frown on music of any kind have lingered long and they have maintained something of a reputation as killjoys that is not really deserved, these days at any rate. We still, however, have some sections of our community who have a very rigid belief in what is and is not acceptable practice; in some parts of the country the idea of doing anything much other than attending church on a Sunday is pretty much frowned on, even now in the twenty-first century. The only problem with this is that such people expect others, not of their own particular persuasion, not just to respect their beliefs but to stick to what they find acceptable. In the old days, though, it was much worse: activities other than attending church, reading the Bible, or perhaps going for a slow walk, were about all that was tolerated.

It so happened that a minister in Fife back in the late 1880s was out for a bit of a constitutional after his first sermon of the day when he came to the house of one of his parishioners, just outside the village. This parishioner was a well-respected man and his skills as a fiddler were in great demand for weddings and other celebrations in the local community. As the minister approached the humble house that day, however, he was mortified to hear the sound of the fiddle being played inside the house. Deeply offended, he marched up to the house and hammered on the door. The fiddling stopped; moments later, the miscreant came to the door, holding his fiddle in his hand.

'David, what was that I was just hearing?' he demanded.

'Och, that was the fiddle, I suppose,' the man replied.

'Do you not know what day it is?' the minister spat out.

'Now, what makes you think I wouldn't know the day of the week, minister?' the fiddler replied, as calm as you like.

At this, the minister became near apoplectic, his cheeks burning red and his eyes almost popping from their sockets.

'David, David, do you not remember the Fourth Commandment?' he roared at the man.

'Naw, Minister, I cannae be sure that I do. But if you care to whistle it, I'll try and pick it up.'

An Unusual Form of Dance

Dancing was very popular all over the Lowland areas of Scotland in the nineteenth century. It was the main form of entertainment for all classes of society and dances were held regularly in towns and villages all over the country. This provided regular work for fiddlers, a considerable number of whom made their living entirely from music. Some combined the role of musician with that of dancing master – teaching youngsters how to do the country dancing so popular at the time – and playing at the dances themselves. Many of them, like Tam Cramb, became noted dancers. Apart from the group dancing, the individual Highland dancing style was considered a particularly manly art, and being a good dancer brought social standing. A well-known fiddler of this period who combined teaching dance with his performances was a man from Stormont, near Blairgowrie, known simply as Dancey Mackenzie. A combination of regular dancing and a love of the outdoors made him a very fit man and, with his great black beard and upright stance, he was an imposing figure. Like many of the other dancing masters of his time, his living was a bit precarious – at certain times of the year there would be plenty work and at others precious little.

Dancey needed some way to supplement his living from music when times were tight. Now, the nineteenth century saw a growth in Highland sporting estates, as Scottish lairds realised they could make considerable revenue from hiring out their shooting rights to 'gentry' from England and even further abroad. This development paralleled the clearances of many areas – it wasn't just sheep that were more profitable than people; deer and game birds like the pheasant, brought in from China, could bring in a respectable income. The fact that birds like the pheasant, virtually hand-reared and not great flyers, make easy targets, has not stopped them still being shot to this day. Many people who were removed from the land, even if only as far as the growing county towns, never forgot where they came from and quite a few of them preserved skills they had learnt living on the land.

One of these skills was poaching and Dancey Mackenzie was one of those who took great delight in supplementing his diet, and probably his income, with birds and game taken from the great estates that surrounded his home village of Stormont. Such poaching, unlike today's generally criminally-organised industrial sabotaging of the countryside, was not only seen as acceptable in many areas, it was also considered to be part of the heritage of any Scot who thought of himself as being descended from Highland stock. In an echo of the ancient independent spirit of the clan warriors, there was a Gaelic phrase that survived throughout the century amongst many who went to the hills. *Fiadh nam Beann, Bradan nam abhain, Fiodh nan Coil* (a deer from the hill, a salmon from the river and fuel from the wood) – these were the three thefts of which a Highlander could never be found guilty!

This saying is thought to have been used by many a poacher with something in his bag when he met one of the estate gamekeepers. It worked as long as the gamekeepers were of local stock, and poachers were primarily taking game 'for the pot', but it became common for the lairds to recruit their gamekeepers from south of the Highland line. It is rather pathetic that often the poachers would be after nothing more than rabbits, which were hardly high on the list of desirable targets for the gentry to shoot.

Then as now, rabbits were a pest, but they did provide a handy source of food for those brave enough to brave the lairds' wrath.

Poachers often used ferrets, called futrets in Scots, a domesticated form of the polecat, an animal known for its ferocity; they were particularly useful for flushing rabbits from their warrens. Dancey Mackenzie was very fond of his favourite ferret; he regularly carried it about him in his clothes and its favourite spot was curled up underneath his great black beard – beards were the fashion at the time and it kept the little futret warm and dry. On more than one occasion, young ladies would miss their steps entirely when dancing and looking up at the imposing figure of the bandleader – only to see the head of a ferret popping out through his beard. Some of those of a delicate constitution were even known to faint at the sight, though many country lasses just laughed at the fiddler.

However, futrets are never more than semi-domesticated; their wild polecat ancestry is never really far from the surface of their behaviour. It happened one night that Dancey was playing at a dance in Rattray, just by Blairgowrie. The hall was packed, a few drams of peatreek had been consumed by the band and the joint was jumping with bonny lasses and fit young men. Dancey was right in the swing of things, playing 'The Mason's Apron' with a great deal of enthusiasm. Suddenly, he let out a roar, dropped his bow and reached under his beard with his right hand. The rest of the band stopped and the dancing ceased. All eyes were on Mackenzie. Eyes glaring and a string of unrepeatable oaths streaming from his lips, the man yanked hard and pulled out the ferret from underneath his beard. And the ferret took some meat with it. It had bitten into Dancey's neck and, like all of its kind, was reluctant to let go. The enraged fiddler threw the creature to the ground, winding it, and, before it could move, he stamped it dead. Many nights after that Dancey Mackenzie had to put up with being asked if he would play 'Footer the Futret' tonight.

May Ye Never Ken A Fiddler's Drouth

This old Scots saying refers to the reputation fiddlers long had for being a hard-drinking lot. In fact, it probably had more to do with the fact that, between sets of music at dances and other social occasions, the fiddlers tended to drink their favourite tipple quickly – before the next set was due to start. Being up in the public eye, such consumption could hardly be hidden. However, there were undoubtedly many fiddlers who liked a drop more than a bit, just like the rest of humanity. One of these was John Brown, a fiddler who was known to fling himself into his work with a great deal of enthusiasm. His love of a party, and his friendly, open-hearted manner, made him very popular at penny weddings, fairs, barn-dances and dancing classes around his home town of Biggar. Ever ready for musical or drinking events, John was known from time to time to get so much into the party spirit that he left the party – or at least his consciousness did.

One night, after spending the day playing and drinking at Biggar fair, John headed home. During the day he had met a good number of friends and acquaintances and the craic had been grand. When he eventually decided to head for home there were several of his friends sleeping the sleep of the innocent at the inn where they had ended up. As it was the annual fair, people had carried on drinking around the comatose party-goers. The sky was just beginning to brighten when John finally made his mind up to go – the fact that the people serving drink at the inn had also fallen asleep might have helped him make up his mind. So off he set, carrying his fiddle and walking with a wee sway, like a sailor home from the sea.

It was just dawn when he hit the road and he was only a mile or so on his way when he was overcome with a dreadful feeling in his guts, a feeling of pain and sickness so bad that he thought his end had finally come. Such events have continued to be the topic of many a musicians' conversation over the centuries, but enough of that. Now, though our John was a man with an open heart and a great capacity for joy, he had been brought up in a strict Calvinist household and the thoughts that assailed him as he was forced to sit by the Biggar road were of hellfire and damnation. The depressive effects of the vast amounts of the whisky and ale he had consumed kicked in with a vengeance. So, there he sat as the brightness of a beautiful summer morning grew around him, shivering, shaking and groaning, expecting every second to be his last and terrified of the judgement he felt sure was imminent. At bottom though, there was a fundamental strength of character in his make-up that always came to the fore and, after half an hour of sitting shaking in misery by the roadside, he launched himself to his feet and shouted to himself, as there was no-one else to hear, and the rabbits in the field would make no sense of what he cried: 'If I have tae dee the day, I'll be as well walkin as waitin.' And he set off on his road. The exercise soon made him feel a little better and by the time he fell into his cottage and collapsed into bed the fear of death had passed him by, but it took a good long sleep and a decent meal before he felt he could face the world. Luckily, he had no engagements for a couple of days after Biggar Fair, having calculated in advance that he might just be wanting to have himself a wee rest after his endeavours.

However, this was hardly the only time our John got the horrors through slaking his fiddler's drouth. On another occasion, suffering similarly, he came to the conclusion that something had to be done. Feeling sorry and offering atonement for his over-indulgent behaviour were not enough. His Puritan upbringing was working overtime and he had reached the conclusion that he should be punished in some way or another. But how to punish himself? The forsaking of the spirit of Old Scotland for a while did not seem to be enough; he felt he needed something more – the Calvinist training of his youth demanded it! The problem troubled him for a few days. Then he turned up at Oggscastle Farm, by Carnwath, farmed by his good friend and sometime drinking buddy, James Paterson. He knocked at the door, of the farmhouse. When Jim came to the door he didn't bother to greet him but blurted straight out, 'Jim, will you let me have a loan of yer gun this mornin? I'm goin tae tak a wee walk doun by Boghall.'

'Faith man, what do you want the gun for?' asked Paterson, recognising by his friend's flushed features, shaking hands and haunted eyes that he was in the grip of fearsome guilt and recrimination.

'You're surely no intendin to shoot yersel, John?' he asked, with a worried frown.

'No exactly, Jim,' came the reply, 'but I surely do intend tae gie myself a good fright!'

Get Your Joke In First

Willie Stewart of Forfar was generally reckoned to be one of the town's finest fiddlers. He was a big lad, over six foot tall and powerfully built. Despite this, he was a gentle, shy soul and when not performing on the fiddle was always a bit backward in company. He was almost a cliché of the notion of the gentle giant and stories were told about his capacity for eating. He dearly loved the local delicacy, the Forfar bridie, a particularly delicious kind of pastie or pie, and was said to have been able to polish off a dozen of these at a sitting when the mood took him! Although he was an intelligent man he was so unsure of himself in company that he had developed a thin skin and often would 'go off in the huff' when comments were made about him, which, truth to tell, was often. In fact, the combination of his great size, his not inconsiderable talents, as both a fiddler and a trencherman, and his colossal shyness made him an easy target for those who considered themselves to be humourists.

This in turn led to stories being told about 'Caups', as he was known from childhood by all and sundry. Caups was a name

145

commonly given to those who liked to lie in their bed of a morning and, truth to tell, Willie's mother had had a hard job dragging him from his bed for much of his childhood. Being the butt of jokes, particularly among those who had a high regard for what they considered their own wit, it is hardly surprising that some of the stories told about Caups were totally untrue. He was just too easy a target and, despite his size, the town 'wits' knew they could get away with saying just about anything about the fiddler. It was situation that caused Willie a considerable amount of annoyance and he resolved to do something about it.

One time, he was coming back to town after playing at a dance in Brechin the night before. It was the middle of winter and snow lay all over the Angus countryside. He came back into Forfar by Tam Clark's Well. This well had a thick stone circular wall round about it and a windlass on the top for hauling up buckets. For a distance of about twenty feet around the well, due to the hardness of the frost, the ground was covered by a sheet of ice which ran straight out over the road there. A bit tired from the exertions of the night before, and with his shoulders hunched against the cold, his hands thrust deep into his pockets, and his head down, Tam was not paying enough attention to where he was going. Just as he approached the well he felt his feet go from him. He flew up in the air and landed on his back with a great doush. Luckily, his fiddle was in its bag around his neck and landed safely on top of his chest. He was badly winded and not a little bruised but he realised that perhaps his chance had come. That night he struggled his way into the local hostelry, where he was due to play. The customers in the bar noted that he was moving very stiffly. Just before he started to play, the big fiddler held up his bow and called for quiet.

This was unheard of! Caups was always reluctant to speak in public. But that night he decided to get his retaliation in first, as he knew some wag or other would soon be making up a story of how he came to be so hurt.

'Well, awbody,' he started, 'A jist thought A shuid tell ye that on ma way back fae Brechin this afternoon A slipped on the ice at Tam Clark's Well. A came down wi such a great doush that all ower the toun folk ran fae their houses, thinkin there was an earthquake.'

This cracked the audience up and was met with rousing cheers as Willie swung into a lively reel. Hs friends, and there were many amongst the crowd there that night, recognised just why he had felt the need to tell the story against himself, and from then on nobody in Forfar made Caups the butt of their humour.

Fiddling and the Kirk

—————◇—————

For many years after the Reformation virtually all forms of dancing, even music itself, were frowned upon. Up until nearly the end of the seventeenth century it was common practice for people found dancing to be hauled before their local Kirk Session and censured, fined or made to sit in the cutty stool in front of the whole congregation during church services. This was an act of public shaming which lasted into the nineteenth century. However, by the early years of the eighteenth century things had eased off somewhat and dancing was well on the way to becoming the universal favourite recreation of all classes in Scottish society, without constant warnings of damnation and hellfire from the pulpit.

Still, in some more out of the way parts of Scotland old habits died hard and there were pockets of what can only be called Puritanism that continued for a long time. Religion has always attracted some characters with an incapacity to understand that others may not see life as they do themselves. There has always been an all too human tendency among certain men of the cloth, and elders of the congregation, to overstretch themselves in their condemnation of others and in their attempts to restrict the natural pleasures of their congregations.

In 1868 a farmer called Peter Clark was denied a certificate of church membership by the Kirk Session of the Free Church congregation at North Knapdale, Argyllshire. This was because the poor man was known to have indulged in the practice of dancing. Now, within the Free Church, which saw itself as the holder of the true flame of Presbyterian Christianity, the withholding of such a certificate was a serious matter indeed. It could even lead to someone being shunned by their local community, so Clark appealed. At the meeting where his appeal was heard the North Knapdale minister maintained not only that dancing was a scandal but that it was 'a flagrant inconsistency in a communicant' and, with typical understatement, 'a sin and bitter provocation to the Lord'. Thankfully, wiser heads prevailed and the reverend gentlemen was unable to find a seconder to uphold the earlier decision.

It wasn't just dancing that could offend such sensitive souls. In 1883 a situation arose in Orkney where fiddling itself was under threat. The minister at Cairston suspended a farmer for the heinous crime of having permitted fiddling to take place at the New Year celebrations in his barn on Deepdale Farm, Stromness. At a time when the world was changing at an everincreasing speed, when travel to all parts of the globe was increasing, and when industrialisation was changing the face of our planet forever, here on a Scottish island a wee group of men had imposed sanctions on one of their number for having allowed the playing of the fiddle in his own premises on the one night of the year when all Scots celebrate. Nowadays the idea of being suspended from a local church would hardly be seen as news, but in those days church attendance was near universal and the idea of being actively prevented from attending the church was a scandalous one. No doubt the minister and his parish council thought they were doing the right thing, but the farmer, John Manson, didn't agree with them.

But the Presbyterian Church is essentially democratic and Manson brought a petition before the presbytery of Cairston to have the decision overturned. Now, in a situation like this feelings were bound to run high and it was decided to hold a meeting of the Joint Kirk Session before the presbytery itself met again. This was, effectively, taking the matter into the public area and at the

Session meeting the conclusion was clear. The presbytery and the Kirk Session were to rescind the decision to suspend John Manson and they were also to remove all references in the minutes both to the original decision and the subsequent petition brought by the farmer. Clearly, the Kirk Session was aware of how ludicrous the situation was and didn't want anyone else to know. But democracy is not something that can be treated lightly and, thanks to someone at the Session, the news leaked out. It is incredible that three hundred years after the Protestant Reformation there were still those in Scotland trying to hold out against music that was not holy.

A Fiddling Minister

There was once in Ayrshire a minister who dearly loved to fiddle. He saw music, his talent for it and dancing as well, as gifts of a bountiful God and was not a man to deprive others of pleasure. This brought him into some conflict with fellow men of the cloth, but that bothered him little. He had been brought up in a musical family and, although he was careful never to play on a Sunday, and not just for fear of offending the more righteous of his parishioners, he spent many an evening in the manse playing for himself, his wife and children. He was a relatively young man; due to his outgoing disposition, sympathetic manners and general happy demeanour, he became very popular amongst the majority of the parishioners. There were a few within the parish who would mutter away to themselves, and each other, about what an example the minister was setting to the young folk, but such people are always with us. Some of these self-defined devout Christians referred to him, with a sniff, as the Fiddlin Minister.

Now, at this time there was a lad in the village called Willie, who had not been blessed with much of the way of sense. Since time beyond counting in most of the world such people, often referred to as naturals, have been seen as in some way touched by God; they were often looked after by the community at large without any necessity of locking them away from the sight of their fellow humans. It is sometimes the way of things that such people, deprived of the normal intelligence, make up for it in strength and energy. Willie was one such and, whenever a task could be found that he could do, he would work like a Trojan till the job was done, or he was told to stop. He was also very fond of music and, whenever he heard anyone playing, he couldn't stop himself from dancing.

One evening, he was passing the manse after the evening mealtime when he heard the minister tuning up. Quickly, he ran to the manse door and knocked. 'Please missis, can I come in an listen to the musics?' he asked the minister's wife when she came to the door – the minister, being of a liberal disposition, did not care to have servants around the house. Janet, the minister's wife, was, like her husband, a kind-hearted soul; she led Willie into the front room, where the minister was now well into 'The Deil Amang the Tailors'. As soon as he was in the room, Willie began to shuffle from one foot to the other and, at a smile from the minister, he began to dance. He certainly had his own style and what he lacked in elegance he made up for in enthusiasm. He began to leap and pirouette around the room with a look of absolute ecstasy on his face. The minister smiled and played on. Whenever he tried to stop, however, Willie looked at him with such a look of pathetic longing that he would launch into another tune. This went on and on till Janet came through again and looked in; her husband was sweating profusely as his visitor leapt around the room with no sign whatsoever of becoming the least bit tired.

At last, though, the minister could not go on.

'Enough, Willie,' he cried, 'I can play no longer.'

Seeing the look of sadness on Willie's face, the now dishevelled minister reached into his pocket for a shilling and handed it to Willie. Before he could say a word, Willie looked at the shilling, then at the minister and said, 'Hoots, minister, the world must be changin affy fast. When I was younger the dancers aye payed the fiddler.'

A Fiddler in the Kirk

Back in the early nineteenth century people were much more religious than they tend to be today. People from all walks of life regularly attended the kirk and it was pretty unusual for anybody not to go. The kirk was in many ways at the very heart of community life in those long-gone days and people actively enjoyed their church-going. Preaching was very popular and a good preacher was guaranteed to get a large audience. It was often noted that, if the preacher was good, people didn't care about the quality of music that accompanied their singing in the least. However, some were more concerned with musical ability than others. In Campsie at the time there was a need for someone to take over organising the singing in the church, the standard of which had been allowed to slip. Luckily, at the time there was a fiddler in the village known for his all-round musical ability. His name was Sandy Norris, and, like many of the men in the area at the time, he was a hand-loom weaver. Though nowadays people remember the radical politics of the weavers of those days, the majority of them were as much Christian as they were radical, in fact usually more so. Sandy was known to be able to sight-read music and had a fine singing voice himself, so he seemed like a good candidate to take over the direction of the music in the kirk. When the minister asked him to take up the post of precentor in the kirk he was happy to oblige. The job of the precentor was to lead the singing and, given Sandy's well attested musical abilities – he had been taking Saturday evening singing classes with the Sabbath School youngsters for quite a while, singing the tune then playing it on the violin to help the bairns pick up the tunes by ear – he seemed to be just the man for the job.

However, there was a wee problem that the minister had not foreseen. Sandy, like most musicians of his time, was well used to playing for dances. The need at the dance was for a sure and steady beat and, given the widespread popularity of dancing amongst the young folk (and many of their elders), and the ready availability of good cheap home-made whisky, the style of dancing tended to be a bit on the fast and furious side. The good old Scottish reels and strathspeys were always at their best at a good canter. So Sandy's musical style had developed with a bit of a beat to it, and this showed itself in his singing. This would probably have presented no problem to the younger members of the congregation, but it was a different story with the older folk. They were used to a style of singing that was in slow time – very slow time. In fact, a lot of it was so dirge-like that many in the congregation had rejoiced at Sandy's appointment, seeing in it a chance to move things along a bit. Their hope was that they would now be able enjoy their singing in the kirk. Added to Sandy's brisk approach to tempo was the fact that he had been introducing new tunes to the Sabbath School – songs that some people wanted to sing themselves. This was all too much for some of the more traditional, meaning elderly, members of the congregation. It all came to a head one Sunday.

A certain Mrs Malcolm grumbled at the end of the service, 'Sandy Norris played sae fest I was aye a double verse behind him.' She was not alone in her complaints and, the following week, a Mr and Mrs George Wallace actually got up and left the church in the middle of the service! This was unheard-of and when Mr Wallace was approached later by the minister he told him, 'Weel, minister, as far as me an the wife are concerned, such-like singing was like being in a theatre and no in a kirk!' This was bitter criticism indeed. When the new parish church was completed soon after, poor Sandy Norris was there as a member of the congregation: a new precentor had been appointed in his place. As one local wag put it, 'Well, they do say the wheels of the Lord grind slow, but no slow enough for Geordie Wallace's singin, it seems.'

Another Sandy Norris Story

One day, while Sandy was still in his position as precentor, the minister was ready for the next psalm and looked over to give Sandy the nod. There was little point in nodding – Sandy was fast asleep, there in the church in front of the entire congregation! The fiddler had been at a wedding the night before and the late night – he had not got home till after four o'clock – and maybe a glass or two of whisky, had ensured that he was not as alert as he should be. The minister was 'black affrontit' and decided to seize the bull by the horns. He grabbed the big Bible from the pulpit; he could just reach down far enough to give Sandy a fierce poke with it. As he nudged the dozing fiddler, he said in a stage whisper that carried to the back of the church, 'Sing, sir, sing.' Sandy, roused dramatically from his slumbers, fair forgot where he was and launched into a rendition of the popular ballad, 'Ye Banks and Braes'. The minister was outraged, as were many of the congregation, and there are those who say this is why Sandy lost his position as precentor. Whether or not this is the case, there was many a night in the rest of his long life that Sandy Norris was stood a glass or two of whisky by his friends, who were ever delighted to tell the tale.

The Social Hour

So many fiddlers made their living over the years at penny weddings and ceilidhs that no collection of fiddling tales would be complete without some particular mention of these vitally important social occasions. As with so many social occasions in Scotland, drink played its part – in some cases far too much drink. As a reminder of just how dangerous that can be, the story of 'Fat Tam's Last Dance' is included here, along with 'The Penny Wedding at Fiddler MacPherson's' and 'A Glen Kitchen Ceilidh'.

The Penny Wedding at Fiddler MacPherson's

William MacPherson, a fiddler in Strathspey, played at many a wedding and barn dance in the early 1800s. He was also quite a successful farmer, owning a considerable amount of land well stocked with cattle. As the years went by and his business prospered, he continued to play the fiddle whenever the occasion presented itself, and this was often at local weddings. There was one wedding, however, at which he took a particularly prominent role. This was the wedding of a friend of his called Francie Moir, who had served in the British army at Waterloo. Before that, Francie had been active in the Peninsular War in the army of the duke of Wellington. After the battle of Waterloo Francie retired and came home to Aberlour, lodging with the widow of a comrade who had fallen in the battle. Meg had been with her man on his and Francie's travels in the Peninsular War,

155

something which was not that unusual in those days. Such camp followers provided a range of essential support services, including helping to look after the wounded. After her husband's death, Meg had returned to Aberlour and bought a pony to set up in the fish business at her cottage in Foggy Boorach. She would take the pony to the Moray Firth ports and return carrying a load of fish, which she would then sell.

She was a hard-working and canny woman and her business prospered. So, by the time Francie returned from the army she had herself a fine cottage, which had a spare room. Francie had no relatives left living in the village and Meg was happy to have company, so the old soldier moved into Meg's spare room. At first there was a bit of gossip about the situation but Francie soon put a stop to that. He was never seen without Old Bess, his gun, and was known to have something of a temper. He terrified the local children, particularly when they came across him drunk on pension day, lying by the roadside with his gun. Whenever he was in his cups he swore something dreadful but, as it was all in Spanish, no one locally knew what he was saying. A remark made by a Buckie lass to her friend at the time perhaps gives a flavour of his speech: 'Oh, lassie, oor Jock cam hame last nicht fae the sodgers. We hardly kennt him, an he speaks sae grand. Oh, Betty ye shuid hear him. His language wuid be beautiful gin it wisnae quite sae sinful.' Our well-travelled ex-soldier soon became a well-known character about the town and, when in funds, after the arrival of his army pension, he was often seen with Fiddler MacPherson in the local taverns. This situation carried on for a few years; then, to everyone's surprise, Francie and Meg announced that they were getting married.

In those days, when money was in short supply for all but the aristocracy and the gentry, the standard wedding arrangements were called Penny Weddings. All the guests would contribute a penny piece towards the celebrations, ensuring that there would be sufficient food, musicians to accompany the dancing and, of course, as much drink as could be bought. Fiddler MacPherson, having been at so many wedding parties, was selected to organise the affair – the fact that he had a substantial barn to hold the event in being something of a bonus, according to Francie. John Mackay, a local weaver, was asked to be the Master of Ceremonies. He had the manners of a gentleman, was very well-read and was the possessor of a blue swallow-tail coat, in which he looked rather grand.

On the morning of the wedding, John turned up to accompany Meg to the church for her marriage. He heard some disturbing news. Francie, no doubt a little nervous, was refusing to come to the church unless he could bring his gun with him. Despite the remonstrations of MacPherson, Mackay and other friends who had assembled for the festivities, old Francie was adamant.

Meg, knowing how stubborn her intended could be, just laughed it off as being of no real importance, and she and John set off for the church. It was here that John Mackay's swallow-tail coat really proved its worth. Apart from the two greybeards, (flagons of whisky) he had in his hands, there were two further bottles in the tail pockets of his coat. He was making sure they would not run short of the good stuff. It was the finest illicit peatreek. It was generally thought that whisky on which no duty had been paid tasted better than officially recognised stuff – and there are those who would still agree today. This pure malt spirit, unlike malt whisky today, hadn't spent many years maturing in wooden barrels – it was probably less than a week old – but was very popular all the same.

So they set off with Meg, resplendent in her brilliant white mutch (a lady's bonnet with scarlet ribbons trailing from it) and a beautiful red and blue silk shawl she had brought back from Spain. On reaching the church, there was Francie – not quite so smart, but over his clothes of homespun hodden grey he was wearing a tail coat. He had Bess in his hand and a belt draped over his shoulder, on which hung his powder horn.

The marriage was set to be performed in the kitchen of the manse, but, when they got there, Francie made it clear he wanted to take his gun in with him. There was more than a suspicion that he and MacPherson had already taken a drink. However, the deacon, Geordie Grant, the local tailor, was having none of it and told him if he wanted to be wed the gun had to stay outside. With further encouragement from MacPherson Francie at last agreed, and the wedding party went into the manse kitchen.

As they entered the manse Francie turned to Grant, saying, 'Haud the mouth o her doun Geordy; I wadna like her tae shoot a tailor.'

Quick as a flash, Geordie replied, 'Och, jist gang awa in, Francie. A doubt but ye'll find the fire o Meg's tongue harder tae staun than fechtin at Waterloo.' Just as the minister started the ceremony there was a noise from the rafters of the kitchen. It was a bevy of doos, or pigeons, cooing and burbling.

Never one to miss an opportunity to make his point, Francie muttered in something like a stage whisper to Meg, 'See. If I'd had Bess wi me, A could soon sort out those doos.'

'Wheesht, Francie, and pay attention,' was her reply.

During the ceremony, Johnny Mackay was passing drams of whisky around those assembled at the manse door, with the help of the local souter, or shoemaker. Then out come the wedding party – Johnny, fired up a bit by the whisky, tried to kiss the bride. He didn't even see Francie move before being felled with a blow from his great fist. As Johnny fell, Francie made to grab Bess but Geordie Grant held it away from him, saying, 'Dinna be daft, ye goukit fool, we'll hae nae shootin here. Johnny has mair sense than you, ye muckle oaf; he kens good breedin. Kissin the bride at a marriage is the custom.'

'Haud aff yer haun,' said Francie, 'or I'll shoot ye baith.'

Again MacPherson had to step in to calm his friend down.

Johnny got back to his feet and shook hands with Francie, who accepted that he wasn't out of order after all, and things carried on. Up on the peat stack, a few of Francie's pals were lined up with muskets of their own and let off a volley in honour of the occasion. Their footing was none too secure and, with the recoil of the weapons, they all tumbled to the ground in front of the newlyweds, to great hilarity all round. Old Francie in particular thought it was very funny and he laughed out loud – which was something that surprised quite a few of the company.

Children from all over the village had arrived for the traditional scramble or 'poor oot', when change was scattered on the ground for them to run after. However, Francie's best man was Lang Charlie Mowat, in whose pockets money never could rest, so there wasn't much for them to scrap over. On the way to MacPherson's farm the company stopped off at the Cottage Inn for a dram or two from Widow Cruickshank. Then it was off for the real festivities, though by this time a few of the company were already well lit up.

Meg's old pal Muckle Nelly stood at the door of the barn with a sieve full of bread and cheese. This was thrown over the bride as she entered, with the traditional cry, 'God gie ye aye plenty meal and claith'. MacPherson had managed to lay his hands on a great copper kettle and a great stew was bubbling away outside the barn. Inside, tables had been laid out in rows and soon the guests were plying their horn spoons with great effect as the stew was handed round with loaves of bread to soak up the gravy. In addition, there were fat hens served with melted butter, curds and creams; and cranachan, a dessert made with oats, cream and a liberal dose of whisky. Francie used his sgian dubh, the traditional small knife of the Highlands, to great effect.

Then the tables were cleared away when the celebrated Strathspey fiddler, John Hay, turned up in his short-tailed tartan coat with his fiddle case tied to the saddle of his shelty, or

Highland pony. He and MacPherson got up on bales of hay at one end of the barn and began to tune up. There were smiles and back-slapping as the crowd formed a ring around the centre of the dance floor for the 'Shemit Reel', the opening dance of the evening performed by the bride, the groom and the bridal party, each of whom pressed a silver coin into John Hay's hands before starting. There was clapping and cheering through the reel; then, at its close, the whole company was up on the floor and the festivities got into full swing.

It was a grand affair and Johnny Mackay, biding his time, got a kiss of the bride unseen by the groom. There were reels and jigs and strathspeys and the barn shook to the thunder of dancing feet. Soon the fiddlers were sweating, and off came their coats. Then there was a short break for the fiddlers' toast, 'May ye never ken a fiddler's drouth.' Fiddlers got very thirsty playing for dances, while other people had the chance to take a drink or two. As the night wore on, off came the fiddlers' neckerchiefs, then the neck studs of their shirts. Then the great Strathspey fiddler was seen at his best – loud and clear with a pulsing rhythm, with MacPherson keeping up alongside him. They played 'Tullochgorum', 'The Haughs o Cromdale' and a host of other popular tunes of the times.

At long last the dancing came to an end and those still standing – there were bodies in a state of collapse all around the barn – accompanied the newlyweds back to Meg's house. There, a few more toasts were drunk and a cry went up for a bedding. This was the old tradition of the bride and groom being carried into the bridal bed and being undressed by their respective companions. It has been suggested that in ancient times this was in fact a custom of witnessing the actual consummation of the marriage by the community. This was too much for Francie. He grabbed Old Bess and stood at the bedroom door as Meg went through, shouting, 'I'll shoot the first man or woman that tries tae get ben the hoose!'

Despite the drink taken, no one was prepared to push things with the newly-wed Francie, whose face and posture made it plain he wasn't joking. So they were left to themselves and the wedding party staggered off homeward.

By this time Willie MacPherson, who had come along to Meg's house, was pretty much the worse for wear. Although his farm was less than two miles away, he lost his way and was seen on hands and knees in a field in front of a scarecrow made up to look like an old woman. He was convinced it was his mother and, staggering to his feet, clasped it in his hands, at which point it broke. He tumbled back into the dreels of the field, where he lay till morning, sleeping the sleep of the just, his arms wrapped protectively round his fiddle.

A Glen Kitchen Ceilidh

Now, ceilidhs can be of all kinds, from a simple gathering of friends where a story or a song is called for and everyone contributes, right through to organised dances with some story-telling and humour thrown in. In the days before radio, record players and television, all of which are recent inventions in the scale of human history, people had to entertain themselves. It had been like that since the very dawn of time for the human species; even today's ceilidhs preserve a degree of continuity with the distant past. Ceilidhs were also the only real social entertainment, other than weddings, that people generally had access to. While dances were frequent in some parts of the country, in areas where the population was limited ceilidhs often took their place. There were, of course, also funerals where celebration could so often go hand in hand with mourning. Many areas had their local Highland Games but they came round but once a year and, particularly in the Scottish winters, there was a need for some sociability to stave off the effects of months of half-light and dreich weather, which always have the tendency to make people depressed. So if there was any occasion that called for a ceilidh, people were delighted. The following story could have happened anywhere.

Organised ceilidhs, to which the local community would be invited, were usually held in the biggest house in the glen. Willie MacGillivray had just such a house with, as was usual, a really big kitchen, which was effectively the living room as well. He had decided to hold a ceilidh to celebrate the engagement of his daughter to the local doctor and invited all his glen neighbours, almost forty all told. He had freshly white-washed the kitchen, made sure that there were plenty peats for the fire, and had a cruisie (a simple oil lamp) set up at each end of the room. It was a moonlit night and the light of the moon coming through the skylight combined with the flickering cruisies to make an intricate and ever-changing play of shadows in the room.

The do was set to kick off at nine o'clock, after people had done their milking and other chores and could devote the rest of the night to enjoying themselves. The night itself was cold and clear with not a cloud in the sky; the stars shone bright over the moonlit landscape. Just before nine o'clock Willie heard the strain of a fiddle coming up the path to his house. This was being played by Rab Fraser, a farmer to trade but weel-kennt for his skill with the fiddle and a very important person for the gathering, leading the guests to Willie's house in traditional style.

As they all entered, many of them carrying even more items of food, and a few more with greybeards and other containers filled with whisky, they each said the words, 'peace be here'. This was replied to by Willie or his wife Jessie with the time-honoured response, 'you're welcome here this night'. As everyone bustled into the kitchen, Rab put down his fiddle momentarily and had a quick dram or two from the bottle in his pocket – he would soon have little time to take another one! The fiddlers were far too busy providing music for celebratory occasions to keep up with other people's drinking. In the olden times people drank amounts of whisky that would frighten a horse these days, and even children regularly took a drop. Given the hard work most people had to do, and the lack of such niceties as central heating and effective draught-excluders in most country homes, the reliance on whisky could be looked on as a necessity.

With a stiffener or two under his belt, Rab was shown to the seat of honour, a chair on a table opposite the door, and things were ready for the off. The room was by now full of men and women of all ages, with a host of the local children there too. There were fit young herd-loons and bonnie milkmaids, stout farmers and their buxom wives, old women in their shawls and old fellows who had only made their way up to Willie's house with the aid of walking sticks. It wasn't just a representative mix, it was virtually the whole glen population. Then, at a nod from Willie, Rab started a reel, the 'Reel o Stumpie'. At the first note a handsome young lass in her mid-teens, Bessie Murray, grabbed the hand of a laddie called James MacIntosh, who had just turned twelve, and hauled him into the space that had been left clear in the middle of the kitchen. His face bright red with embarrassment, the lad was led off into the dance, his first ever with a grown woman. This was met with cries of encouragement and soon the floor was filled with dancing couples.

The dancing went on for twenty minutes until a break was called. At this point everybody sat where they could around the kitchen, some on chairs, some on benches and many of the younger ones on bales of straw Willie had brought in from the barn to serve as seats. One after another, local men and women told stories and jokes interspersed with songs, sometimes accompanied by Rab on the fiddle. There were ghost stories to frighten the bairns, tales of whisky makers outwitting the excisemen and a variety of songs, several from the pen of Robert Burns.

After a while, Jessie and her two eldest daughters began to lay out food on the long farmhouse table set against the wall

Covered with a home-made cloth tablecloth, bleached as white as the finest linen, the table was then heaped with food. There were plates of boiled and roasted hens, bowls of skirlie (a combination of fried onions and oatmeal) and others of potatoes with heaped-up piles of oatmeal and barley cakes. There was also a side of ham, a couple of roasts of venison – even a couple of poached salmon. Greybeards of the local peatreek, the finest whisky in the world according to local taste, were placed among the food. Willie had had a prosperous couple of years and wanted to celebrate in style. Everyone helped themselves and the grand repast was washed down with buttermilk by the bairns and whisky, or water, by the adults.

When the eating was done, the table was cleared and all sat in a circle for more tales. Stories of great heroes were followed with stories of how cleverly fairies had been outwitted; time and again people told tales they had told a hundred times before. One local woman of advanced years told the eerie tale of the banshee who came to tell of impending death. She was followed by her husband, who told the story of the kelpie, or water horse, that was said to live near the bridge down the glen. Children and adults sat entranced as the stories unfolded.

Then it was time for the dancing to start again and Rab struck up a tune as the dancers took to the floor. It was more than an hour before the poor fiddler got a break. Then there was a round of jokes and riddles. By now, the youngest of the children were asleep or had been taken home and the bawdiness of the material was notable. Also one or two of the young lads and lasses had disappeared into the night together; the age-old way of things went on, as ever it does.

Then it was into the last few dances. The very last reel had to have Willie and Jessie taking part, but by now more than a few of their neighbours were snoring in corners. Then the ceilidh was over and Rab led those still standing back down the glen to their various homes, playing 'Lord Reay's March'. It has to be said that Rab's playing was a bit slurred; by now it was well past three in the morning. However, like all of his neighbours in those far-off days, Rab was up by seven in the morning and setting about the day's darg on his farm. They played hard and worked hard in those days.

Fat Tam's Last Dance

In the modern world we often see newspapers getting themselves in a lather about the over-consumption of alcohol, particularly among the young. This is nothing new. In the late eighteenth century in Scotland drink was consumed in fierce amounts. Whisky was the favoured drink for many of the common people and even children of five and six were known to 'take a dram'. However, the worst of the imbibers were probably the lairds, the landowning aristocracy, and the judges, who tended to come from the landowning class themselves. Some would say not much has changed. There is a story told of a fiddler in the Borders at this time; it might serve as an illustration.

Now, the fiddler was Sandy Graham, who had been born in the shadow of Tinto Hill, near Biggar, the site of ancient pagan practices. Its name, supposedly from the Gaelic *teinteach*, means firetop. Now Sandy, like many of his profession at the time, was forced to travel the countryside playing at farmtouns and at dances and weddings wherever he could find them. In those days the farmtouns were like communal farms; a group of families each had their own piece of land near to the township, which was surrounded by common grazing lands where wood could also be collected. The system was pretty basic and provided not much above a subsistence living; in many ways it was akin to the crofting system further north. Like the crofting system, at the back of it were the lairds, large landowners who often modelled themselves on the English upper classes, forgetting their ancestry was essentially no different from the humble cottars to whom they leased their lands.

Some of the lairds were, of course, decent human beings but some used their power over their tenants like medieval despots. And some of them were known to spend their rents on a great deal of self-indulgence. One of these was the laird of Haughside, an estate to the south of Tinto. This man was an out-and-out tyrant and treated his servants and tenants with absolute disdain. Times were hard then and being thrown off one's land or out of one's job could easily result in starvation; the laird of Haughside took full advantage of this to bully and harass his tenants. Now, Sandy knew all about Fat Tam, as the laird was generally known around the countryside, and had even seen him at one or two of the balls he had played at in the big houses in the area. He had no personal knowledge of the man and had no wish to get to know him. His drinking was legendary throughout the Borders and, though Sandy was as fond of a drink as the next man, he had no wish to come near Fat Tam.

However, things don't always work out to our satisfaction and one of Sandy's cousins, Isobel, was taken on as maid at Haughside. Now, Sandy had long been fond of Isobel and realised that she must have been in pretty desperate straits to take on such a job. Sure enough, when he came to visit her when next he was in the area, he found she had fallen on hard times, her previous employer having died and his children having sold up the family estate and moved to London. The new owners had brought their own servants and Isobel had lost her job as assistant housekeeper. Here she was back to working as a humble maid in one of the worst houses in Scotland. The housekeeper herself was a vicious bully and she would have sent Sandy packing as soon as she saw him, but for one thing – his fiddle. Mrs McGinnis might have been a hard-hearted harridan but she had always loved the fiddle. So when Sandy called on his cousin he was invited in, given food and poured a glass of whisky. Mrs

McGinnis asked if he would regale them with a tune, preferably something from her homeland of Ireland, she said, but she was sure he would play something nice for them. Aware that agreeing would likely make his cousin's life a bit better, Sandy was happy enough to play a tune or two. He had also noticed that one of the maids, a fine buxom, fair-haired lass had given him a smile as he had arrived, and he liked the look of her.

So he played an old Irish air, an air which brought a tear to the cheek of the housekeeper. This was something unexpected amongst the rest of the staff and he was encouraged to play a bit more. His glass was refilled and Sandy launched into a fine old reel. The staff were delighted with the unusual prospect of a bit of cheer in the Haughside kitchen and when Mrs McGinnis allowed the bottle to be passed around they were beside themselves. This was a remarkable day indeed.

After a few tunes the atmosphere in the kitchen began to seem like a ceilidh. Sandy had arrived in the late afternoon and, by nightfall, the kitchen was in full swing. Sandy had by now found out that the buxom maid's name was Nancy and he was watching her closely as she danced with one of the manservants. She seemed to be aware of his interest and kept smiling at him as she whirled around the room. Suddenly a bell rang; several of the servants who had been dancing just a moment before fled from the room. Sandy stopped in mid-tune, his bow upraised as Mrs McGinnis got to her feet and gave herself a shake. Isobel put her fingers to her lips to tell the fiddler to keep quiet, and she too left the room. The housekeeper took the bottle of whisky from the table and replaced it in a cupboard. The few servants who remained in the kitchen were immediately busy, fetching a tray and food and several bottles of claret from another cupboard. These were whisked off out of the kitchen with some speed.

Within minutes, one of the manservants had returned to the kitchen.

'The laird wants a word with Sandy, Mrs MacGinnis,' said the man, looking sideways at the housekeeper.

'What?' she demanded, her normal personality having returned with the sound of the bell.

'He said that he heard the music and the laughin and he wants us all to go upstairs, Mrs McGinnis,' the man replied, looking anxious.

'What do you mean, all of us?' she asked with a quizzical look.

'That's just what he said; he wants the fiddler and the rest of us to go upstairs to the main hall,' the man insisted.

So Sandy found himself trooping upstairs to the main hall, to see all the servants assembled in front of the gross figure of Fat Tam himself. A couple of his cronies were sitting in chairs against a wall. The great lump of a laird had a pint pot of claret in his hand and as soon as Sandy entered the room he let out a roar.

'There ye are ye, half-starved wretch! Come on then, play us a tune – a reel – and let's get them dancing. That's what you were all doing in my kitchen, weren't ye?' he roared at the lined-up servants. Mrs MacGinnis curtseyed and nodded.

'Well then,' he yelled again, 'get playin, fiddler. You'll get paid. And you lot, you lot get dancin. It'll do me good tae see ye aw dance and enjoy yersels. McPherson, fill the punch bowl and pass it round.'

Sandy, at first, had no intention of obeying this gross poltroon, but then he thought of Isobel and Nancy; he was more than a little interested in the fair-haired lass. If he didn't do what this great oaf demanded it could be rough on them. So he launched into a vigorous reel and the servants all began to dance, stopping as MacPherson passed around them with two great pitchers of punch, which seemed to have appeared from nowhere. In reality, the servants could always supply a ready-prepared punch bowl, being well-used to their employer's dissolute habits.

As the servants whirled around, the laird stood in the middle of the room, taking great pulls on his glass and shouting at the top of his voice.

'Drink up, lads and lasses! Dance, dance like the demons ye are. Drink. Drink until ye're aw fou. Drink as much as ye like – the mair ye drink the better ye'll be.'

As he raved in the middle of the floor his cronies in the corner pointed at the servants and laughed, well aware that the hired help were not enjoying the occasion. And all the time they were quaffing away at the punch themselves. Soon the big wash tub from downstairs was hauled up at the laird's insistence, and into it went all the makings for a super-toddy. Several gallons of brandy were followed by more gallons of hot water, pounds of sugar and bags of lemons, imported from far away at great cost.

'Drink up, drink up,' he cried, 'drink up or get out of my hoose this instant. I'll have no damn sobersides in Haughside the night!'

Fat Tam had returned to his home in his usual state of drunkenness and, in this condition, he possibly thought he was being generous to his servants. After all, which of them could afford to drink brandy toddies unless he paid for them? His drink-impaired mental faculties and his bullying nature led him to think he was some kind of philanthropist. What other Border laird would treat his servants this way?

Some of the younger maids couldn't hold their liquor and up it came. But Fat Tam was still on his feet and simply made them drink more, sending to the cellars for wine and brandy and whisky as soon as he thought things were slowing down. And all the time Sandy kept fiddling for the dancers. When the drunken buffoon remembered that the fiddler needed a drink too, he would stagger over and hold a cup to Sandy's mouth while he played on.

And all the time Fat Tam made sure McPherson kept pouring more and more drink and shouted to the servants to dance. After a couple of hours of this, one by one they began to wilt. One or two collapsed in corners, retching miserably, before falling into a stupor. Others just kept drinking till they fell down dead drunk. Soon there were bodies littered all over the hall. McPherson the butler passed out just as he was carrying another jug of punch to the laird. The jug fell from his hand, and the contents spilled across the floor as the jug smashed on the bare wooden floor-boards. And still the laird raved on. Soon there were only Fat Tam, Sandy and two of the young servant lads still drinking. Everyone else had passed out and was fast asleep. Then the two young lads collapsed in a heap. One tried to stagger back to his feet but, try as he might, his legs were like rubber and he collapsed asleep next to his pal. By this time, with no one else to force drink on, the laird was constantly holding the cup to Sandy's mouth, by now heedless of his shirt and breeks sodden with the amount that had been spilled. He was 'roarin fou'. He had been missing notes and misbowing for a good while but still Fat Tam cried for more.

The laird staggered towards the big tub, still half full of punch, due to its having been filled three or four times in the course of the evening – nobody could be sure. Then Sandy, realising he could hardly play a note, staggered to his feet, dropping his fiddle on the floor. In a state of total inebriation, he barely heard the laird shout once more, 'Dance, dance like a demon, man.' Unthinkingly, Sandy began to lurch about in a sorry imitation of a dance. He had no idea where he was really, never mind where his fiddle was. Inevitably he staggered, once, twice and a third time. His right foot came right down on the fiddle! There was a horrible noise of breaking strings and splintering wood. Somehow the horrific sound pierced the fog of drink in his brain and he stood straight up, suddenly aware of what he had done to his pride and delight, his fiddle. As that horrible realisation came upon him Sandy too passed out.

Hours later, with the sun well up in the sky, Sandy vaguely heard the sounds of birds singing in the trees outside Haughside.

His head was ringing as if it was inside a cathedral bell and his mouth felt as if a nest of rats had been sleeping in it. He moved and at once felt so sick he groaned. He opened one eye. The room swam before him in a scene of devastation. Bodies were collapsed all round the room; everywhere there were pools of drink and everywhere there was vomit. Moaning quietly to himself, he opened his other eye and got to his knees. There in front of him was his fiddle, the neck broken clear off and the body caved in its entire length. Sandy let out a dreadful groan. This caused a body lying near him to move. As Sandy knelt there, a look of horror on his face as he gazed on his fiddle, MacPherson the butler climbed slowly to his feet.

'Oh, no. Oh my God, no!' Sandy heard him say.

'Aye, it's dreadful richt enough. I've ruined my fiddle, my poor wee fiddle,' replied Sandy, tears beginning to flow from his red-rimmed eyes.

'Nnnn . . . Nnnn . . . No, not your fiddle. Look.' The butler was pointing over to the big tub that had fuelled so much of the dissipation of the night before.

There, head first in the tub was Fat Tam! He had gone for yet more drink when Sandy passed out and his foot had slipped on the floor; he had gone head first into the still half-filled tub. Too drunk to move and having driven all his servants to a state of collapse, there had been no one to help the obese laird up out of the impromptu punch bowl, and he had drowned.

Sandy and MacPherson rushed over and managed to haul the great lump of flesh out of the bowl, but it was to no avail: he was long dead. Afterwards it was said in all the area around that it had been a fitting way for Fat Tam to go, swimming in a bowl of punch. A cousin of his inherited the estate and turned out to be a half-decent human being, so Isabel stayed on and in time became housekeeper herself. As for Sandy – well, he managed to have his fiddle repaired and it sounded almost as good as ever. When he told the story in later years he always said that it was an ill wind that blew no good. He had ended up convincing Nancy to become his wife. But if anyone ever suggested he might like a glass of punch he would turn white at the very thought of Fat Tam's Last Dance.

A Couple o Lads o Pairts

A recurring hero of Scottish culture is the Lad o Pairts. This refers to men who are talented in several ways and might even have more than one career at the same time. It reflects an ongoing part of Scottish culture, which has always valued the generalist approach. These individuals are usually presented as having come from rather limited backgrounds, but this usually means their families were not financially well off. In this there is an aspect of the dour side of the Scottish character, which shows itself in sayings like, 'hard work never killed anybody'. The two stories here are about men who certainly worked hard, but who in their intellectual reach and inquisitive reasoning were fine examples of the ideal of the Lad o Pairts.

The Bed-ridden Fiddler

John Smith was a farmer near Blairgowrie, a man who enjoyed music and a fiddler of some renown. One night, early in the 1840s, he was in the Losset Inn in Alyth to play a few tunes with some friends. John was at this time in his mid-fifties, as were two of the others there, James McGovern and Tam Stewart. They too were local men, as was the youngest man in the company, Jamie Speed, who was barely in his twenties. The fifth man was called Alex Stevenson; he hailed originally from Dundee and had moved into the area to set up as a feed merchant a few years earlier. He was in his forties. John was just taking his fiddle out of its case when one of the company said, 'Tell us how you got that fiddle there, Johnnie.'

'Ah, well,' said John, 'there's a story and a half in this fiddle, I'll tell you.'

'Well then, dinnae keep it to yoursel,' chipped in Stevenson, who hadn't heard the tale before.

Taking a sip from his glass on the table, John wiped his lips with the back of his hand and said, 'It was a few years ago and I was at a roup up at the head o Glen Shee. I wasnae looking for anythin in particular but I'd known the fairmer wha had been there an was just kind o interested for auld times sake. Anyway, towards the end I hadnae actually bought oniethin when a big wicker basket came up. Now, the mannie in charge o the auction just said it was full o assorted domestic goods, but it was a fine basket, about three foot across and half o that deep. So I started the biddin and got the thing for a tanner. Well, I had a quick look in it. There were a few auld pots and pans and some stuff tied up wi bits o paper and I thought I'd hae a good look when I got back to the hoose.'

At this point he stopped and took another sip of whisky.

'Ye ken, though, how things work oot. I was just back hame when the wife came after me tellin me a man had been round tae look at some stots I had for sale and had left his address. So what wi that an one thing an another I just put the basket in the back o the shed at the back door an forgot all about it. It must hae been three weeks later when I happened to notice it and, as it was a right rainy day, I thought I might as well empty it out. So I opened it up and started pullin things oot. As I said, there were some pots and pans, a bunch o horn spoons wrapped up in paper, some bone-handled knives, broken butter pats and a bunch o other stuff. Well, I put them all on the floor and looked deeper into the basket.'

He paused and looked around the four other men at the table.

'There, at the bottom of the basket, covered wi dust, was a fiddle case. And no just any fiddle case; I recognised the style o the case, right aff. It was made wi Alyth pine, ye can aye recognise the redness o it, tho there's no much left o it these days.' Again he took a sip of whisky and looked around the group, smiling and his eyes twinkling. 'I didnae even have tae open it tae ken what was inside. It was one o James Sandy's cases and I was sure that the fiddle would be one o his as weel. So I opened it up an there it was. A mint-condition fiddle fae the hand o James Sandy, the Alyth genius.'

At that he lifted the fiddle and burst into a quick few bars of 'The Deil Amang the Tailors'.

'It's a braw fiddle, right enough,' said Stevenson. 'That's a real good tone it has. But who was this James Sandy?'

The four others fell over each other to tell him all about James Sandy, the Alyth genius.

James Sandy was born in the Strathmore town of Alyth in 1766 and was the son of a local master joiner. He was a bright and active lad, who from a very early age showed himself to be adept with all kinds of tools and was possessed of a clear musical gift. He was sent to music lessons as a wee lad and by the time he was in his teens was already a good fiddler. Then something happened which changed his life for ever. It was midwinter a heavy frost had fallen and the local lochs were all frozen over. This provided the local children and young people with a great opportunity for skating, and the men of the area with the chance to indulge in a bit of curling. James and a bunch of his pals went out with their home-made skates to have some fun on the Loch of Lintrathen, a few miles to the northeast of Alyth. Now, the Loch of Lintrathen is a fair size and this meant that you could get up a decent head of speed on skates. So there they were, with loads of others skating around, and James was getting faster and faster, weaving in and around slower skaters. But frozen lochs, unlike modern ice rinks, aren't smooth. James was hurtling along when his right skate hit a ridge in the ice; he flew up in the air and fell with a sickening crunch on his back.

He was unable to move and had to be carried all the way back to Alyth, where he was put to bed. The local doctor came and could do nothing, other than make the young lad comfortable. He then had the sorry task of telling James's parents that their son had badly damaged his spine and it was highly unlikely that he would ever walk again. For most people this would have been a tragedy. But not for James. He was installed by his parents in the first floor front room of their house, overlooking the Losset Burn that runs through Alyth. Today the building is the Commercial Hotel and it was here that James spent the rest of his life.

And what a life it was. Restricted to his bed he might have been, but that was the only restriction that James Sandy would allow. He continued to play music and read every book he could lay his hands on. He also devoured every newspaper and magazine he could get and made a point of keeping up with what was happening in the world beyond Strathmore. It was important to him to know what was happening in India and America and in far-off Australia. His body might have been confined to a single room in the wee Strathmore town of Alyth, but his mind and his imagination roamed the world.

The remarkable thing about James was that he became a truly superb artificer. His legs might be of no use to him, but his hands and his brain had nothing wrong with them. He had a table built on pulleys, which raised or lowered it over his bed. He had racks of different tools round his bed and even a small forge installed in his bedroom at a later date. And, within a few years, he showed that he had learned a great deal from his father; but he was more than a joiner, even a master joiner. He also appears to have been something of a mechanical genius. He could turn his hand to making just about anything.

He turned out telescopes, for which he ground the lenses himself, snuff boxes, music boxes, fishing rods, decorative dirks and swords, pocket knives, bird cages, horn spoons, candlesticks – virtually any small thing in metal or wood. He was also adept at making and repairing watches and clocks and his skills were known and valued through a wide area of Angus and Perthshire.

But James was also a highly sociable character and this, combined with his love of music, meant that his bedroom overlooking the square at Alyth became the social centre of the wee country town. Here all the news from the locality and from further afield was discussed. The ideas of the radicals who were demanding parliamentary reform caused many a heated a discussion, as did the new ideas in philosophy, engineering and exploration that were going the rounds. Such was his fame that it was with great regret that Robert Burns missed visiting him when the bard came up to Forfar in 1787.

His love of music and his wonderful skill with his hands made it almost inevitable that James would turn his talents to making fiddles. His fiddles were very much sought-after in the area, for, although he had to rely on others to source the material for his violins, his creative skills were first class. Many a night of fine music was heard in his room; he played with the throngs of musicians who beat a path to his door from many parts of Scotland to buy a fiddle and to meet the Alyth genius. As was the norm in most of Scotland, on such nights there would be a large greybeard of peatreek, sitting on a sideboard in his room, just to help oil the wheels of social intercourse.

He also had a sense of humour, our bed-bound fiddler. One day his friend Willie Duff was visiting. Now, Willie had been blind from birth but, like a lot of other people, used the words 'I see' quite a lot. One day, after a visit and a wee drappie or two, Willie was taking his leave of James, who had been playing a few tunes. James said, 'Well, I hope you'll be back to see me soon then, Willie.' Willie wasn't daft himself and caught the point.

'Och aye, Jamie, A'll be back tae see you and we'll hae a bit walk thegither then.' This brought gales of laughter from the rest of the company. After what was by any standards a full and happy life, James died in 1819. His good-heartedness was obvious right to the end, for he married his long-term house-keeper just three weeks before his death to make sure that she would be comfortably off for the rest of her days.

As John Smith finished the story of James Sandy that night in the Losset Inn, his friends seemed stricken with the onset of colds; there was a bout of blowing into handkerchiefs and coughing.

'Aye,' said John, 'I was lucky enough tae be at a few memorable musical evenings in James Sandy's hoose when I was young lad, but I never thocht I would end up wi ane o his fiddles. As soon as he made one there was always somebody ready to pay for it. But I couldnae have got a better one.'

And he raised the fiddle and played a slow air that let the smooth, round tone of the instrument sound to best effect. After that, they all got their fiddles out and another fine night's playing was under way in Alyth's Losset Inn.

Another Fiddler o Pairts

Girvan in Ayrshire used to have a fiddler of some repute in the early 1800s. His name was Alexander McCallum and, being over six foot tall, he was known in the district as Lang Sandy. He trained to be a weaver, just like his father before him, but by the time he had grown to manhood the independent weavers were a dying breed. They couldn't compete on costs with the new factories, which produced cloth that was flooding the market, and so Sandy had to turn to another trade. Luckily for him, he had shown an early ability for music and had been taught to play the fiddle. There was widespread demand for fiddlers, and musicians playing in the streets of villages and towns were common. Due to his natural musical gifts, allied to a considerable intelligence and an enquiring mind, Sandy soon developed a reputation as a fine exponent of the bow and became one of the most popular of the fiddlers in and around Ayrshire, regularly being asked to play at weddings and dances. As we know, in the old days people worked extremely hard and, in consequence, they played hard whenever they got the chance. In those times, a six-day week was the norm and holidays were very few and far between. This meant that social occasions like weddings were keenly anticipated. It was also common at weddings and dances for people to dance throughout the night and head off to their work in the morning. Fiddlers, though, had finished their work with the last dance, and could head home to bed.

One morning about seven o'clock, Sandy was heading home when he was met by an old pal, Jimmy Purgavie, a carpenter, on his way to work at the nearby boatyard. Purgavie saw at once by Sandy's rolling gait and look of bemusement that his friend was a wee bit the worse for wear with the drink. In fact he looked guttered!

'Hello there, Sandy. You've a richt skinful on ye. Where hae ye been?' he asked.

Sandy stopped and focused on his friend. 'Ach, it's yourself Jimmy. It's a fine bright morning, is it no? Would ye like a drink?' Saying this, he brought a bottle from the deep pocket of his coat and held it out. It was empty.

'Na, na, it's a bit early for me,' laughed the carpenter. 'Just put it awa. A was askin whaur ye were last nicht,' he went on.

'Last nicht, last nicht,' mused Sandy, swaying a bit as he stuck the empty bottle back in his pocket and tried to focus his thinking.

'Well, I tell ye, Jimmy, I dinnae ken if it was a waddin or a funeral, but I had a rare time. Good nicht.' And, with that, the fiddler staggered home to his bed.

Now, while Sandy was undoubtedly in demand for weddings and dances, these didn't happen every week, and playing in the streets could be a bit hit and miss in terms of a steady income. So Lang Sandy decided to turn his hand to making fiddles. This was not that uncommon in those days, the popularity of the fiddle meaning there was always a demand for instruments of all levels of quality. In learning to be a weaver he had been shown how to fix and maintain looms, so he was conversant with the use of tools. In those days many people were adept at repairing and fixing all sorts of things and it wasn't unusual to be good with one's hands at all. So Sandy, by dint of experiment and reading a few books, quickly learned to turn out a good fiddle. Soon he was being given instruments to fix and restore. Some of these were quite old instruments and Sandy, of course, knew a good fiddle when he saw one.

So from there it was logical step to start dealing in old fiddles and, before he knew it, he was buying and selling other old bits and pieces such as furniture and clocks, finding himself in what was then known as the antiquarian business – what we now would call antique dealing. Even back then, people who had a bit of spare cash were often interested in buying what they considered antiques – objects from far-away countries and military memorabilia being particularly popular. As a man with an inquiring mind and capable hands, Sandy was always up to something; along with his increasing prosperity came the unusual and welcome advantage of having time on his hands. His business was going so well he was able to pick and choose what gigs he would play and he began to nourish the idea of becoming an inventor. There was, of course, a great interest in all aspects of science and many people thought that progress was an unstoppable and totally benign force.

As a man of his times, Lang Sandy MacCallum subscribed to this notion; he even designed a torpedo boat, though there is no record of its ever being built. His inquiring mind led him into more and more areas of interest and he took a particular liking for geology, at this time a science that was still in its infancy. In the course of his studies he met the most famous geologists of his day, including Hugh Miller and Roderick Murchison, who even went so far as to name a Silurian fossil after him. From being a weaver, Sandy took up the fiddle, which led to him being first a fiddle-maker, then a fiddle dealer, and then an antique dealer. He ended up mixing with some of the greatest minds of the Victorian era, but was still to be found on occasion leading the dancers at weddings and balls in Girvan.

The Fiddle and the Jail

Although James MacPherson of Rant fame certainly appears to have been little more than a freebooter, a euphemistic term for an armed robber, there are other stories concerning fiddlers and jail. Considering how long the fiddle has been an integral part of Scottish culture, it is not to be wondered at that now and again one or other 'brother catgut' would fall foul of the law. Again, as in other types of story, we have both happiness, in 'The Power of the Fiddle' and in 'Key Use of a Fiddle', and sadness, in the story of the tune 'Jack Broke the Prison Door'. The first story here also shows that tales can be carried to the ends of the earth, and others can come back from there.

The Power of the Fiddle

In the early years of the nineteenth century, a great many Scots emigrated to different parts of the world. The Highland and the Lowland clearances saw people uprooted from the lands where their ancestors had lived for centuries and dispersed to far-flung parts of the British empire, often to help in the process of displacing people who had themselves lived on their own lands for centuries. One place where many Scots ended up was New Zealand. The Land of the Long White Cloud had beautiful mountains and tumbling rivers and was in some ways like Scotland. It was also a place that could be economically exploited, once the native Maori peoples had been subdued. After the first settlers had cleared away the dense forests, the land was perfect for raising sheep. It was ironic that many Highlanders cleared from Scottish glens to make way for sheep ended up working on great sheep farms on the other side of the world, on lands once inhabited by the natives there. In the early days, before the infrastructure of a modern state could be built, it was a rough and ready place, and the justice was rough and ready too. The crime of sheep-rustling was seen as a threat to the very existence of the fragile communities being set up in virtual wilderness areas. It had to be treated severely; there were often no official law officers and people effectively created their own local laws.

One man who had come out from Scotland was Sandy McMorran, a man with no great farming skills, but known to be a fair fiddler. In those distant days, when there was little entertainment of any kind available in the isolated communities, musicians were always popular. And, as one of a community well outside the reach of government control, he had agreed with the rest of the community on the laws that should be upheld. This included the laws concerning sheep-rustling.

Sandy, who mainly worked as a labourer, fell on hard times and made the mistake of nicking one of his neighbour's sheep. As the man had several thousand of the beasts, Sandy didn't think one would be missed; and anyway he was hungry. However, in small isolated communities it is difficult to get away with anything; Sandy was caught and tried for sheep-stealing. Now, in those days the local town consisted of very few buildings: a few houses, maybe a school, a shop or two, three or four barns and the local grog-shop, or liquor shanty. Given little alternative, this was where the local court was held and justice was dispensed, along with hard liquor. Sandy knew what was in store for him. The penalty for sheep stealing was very clear: death by hanging.

It was with glum faces indeed that the locals picked a judge and jury to try Sandy. They really had no choice; the law was clear and had the agreement of the entire community. Generally, such laws were thought to be applicable to outsiders passing through, or bandits, but Sandy was guilty; he didn't deny it, and the only sentence was for him to go to the halter.

The gathered men of the area were downcast. They all knew Sandy and liked him. Yet they also knew that they had to have some law and that all had agreed what the law should be. There was no alternative. They had no jail and, anyway, the law was explicit. Into this gloomy atmosphere, as they were contemplating the actual mechanics of hanging Sandy, a voice was raised.

'Afore we do anythin else, let's have a drink,' said the man whose sheep Sandy had stolen.

There were immediate sounds of agreement from the assembled company.

'We'd better let Sandy hae one as weel,' said another, and this too was met with general agreement.

So the owner of the grog-shop was told to give everyone a drink, which would come out of the local taxes. Well, one thing leads to another, as my granny always used to tell us, and another drink was poured and drunk. After the third drink – the drams they drank in those days being of a much larger size than the government-approved trickles we get today – one or two of them were beginning to relax.

The local blacksmith, John Farquhar, liked his drink and when he drank he liked to dance. 'Right,' he said, standing up at the table he was sitting at, 'I think we should get Sandy to give us a wee tune. After all, it's the last time we'll get the chance to hear him play.'

This too met with general agreement and Sandy, a wee bit warmed up with the drink, and anxious to put off his execution for as long as he could, was in total agreement. So his fiddle was sent for; meanwhile they all had another drink. The fiddle arrived and a space was cleared in the middle of the floor. Sandy stood on a table against the wall and launched into the 'Reel of Tulloch'.

Immediately, Farquhar and a bunch of others were on the floor, dancing away merrily. The tune was followed by another reel. Then a Strathspey, then another reel, then a jig. By this time the joint was jumping! Men were hooching great style and the few ladies who lived in the small community had been brought in to add a bit of taste and colour to the proceedings. Those who weren't dancing were tapping their feet as they sipped at their whisky. And, with the effects of the drink, people began to reminisce of Scotland. Alex Shand, the local carter, who had originally come from Gala in the Borders, called out, 'Sandy, could you play us 'The Flooers o the Forest'?'

Luckily, Sandy knew the tune and, as the famous lament was played, there was many an eye that had a tear in it, thinking of the old country.

At this point, two of the men who had been part of the jury went to a third and started whispering in his ear. Just then, Sandy finished, to total silence. Before anything else could happen he launched straight into another reel. Up got the dancers and they were off again. But this time some of them were being pulled off the floor by the two jurors. One after another, those who had sat on the jury were taken to one side. Each time the same thing was said: 'Do you no think it would be an awful thing to dae awa wi Sandy?'

The jurors in a group then went to where Pat Donachie, the appointed judge, was sitting slumped in a chair, half asleep. Giving him a stiff nudge, the two leading jurors spoke sharp and quick to him.

He sat bolt upright, looked around him and listened to what they had to say. As soon as they finished, he pushed his way through the dancers to the table that Sandy stood on.

'Stop, in the name of the law,' he cried.

Sandy, his heart in his mouth, stopped playing. The dancers stopped dancing. There was complete silence as everyone waited for what was going to happen next.

'Help me up, man,' the judge said to Sandy, putting up his hand. Sandy took the hand and pulled the man up. As he did so, the whisky wore off in a flash and he stood there beside the judge, his face white and his body beginning to shake.

'Right, everybody,' called Donachie, 'The court is back in session.'

He turned to Sandy.

'Sandy McMorran,' he intoned solemnly, 'do you swear on your life and on the Holy Bible that you will never again steal the sheep of any man?'

The crowd took a deep breath as one. Sandy, feeling afraid and not really understanding what was going on, replied, 'Aye, aye, I'll swear to that.'

Donachie held up his hand again as people began to mutter and ask questions.

'Wheesht!' he shouted. 'By the power invested in me by the court I hereby revoke the sentence of hanging and tell you, McMorran . . .' at this point he stopped and looked round the whole company. 'I say again, Sandy McMorran, I tell you, it's time you were playing us another tune.' At that, he jumped off the table to cheers, laughter and joy from all there. Sandy, his eyes bursting with tears, was almost unable to play. Almost. At heart, he was a true musician and he swung into another tune as the company stumbled onto the dance floor.

The party continued through till the next morning and, before it was over, a collection had been made for Sandy. It raised enough for him to set himself up as a carter. He continued to play the fiddle at weddings and dances all around the area; every time he did so, somebody would tell the tale of how the Fiddler Escaped the Gallows.

Key Use of a Fiddle

This story took place in a Scottish town some time around the turn of the nineteenth century. It was a prosperous town, with a busy port and a good trade with the hinterland; like most towns of the time, it was effectively run by the baillies who sat on the town council. In the centre of the town, by the river that ran through it, was the local prison. This was on the upper floor of a substantial stone building and consisted of two main cells: one for thieves and other criminal miscreants, and the other for debtors. In those days it was hardly uncommon for people to be locked up for being unable to pay their bills and many an honest man, fallen on hard times, found himself suffering the ignominy of spending a while behind the bars of the debtors' prison.

One of these at the time was a young lad called James Fleming, aged twenty-two years and of what was generally considered a good family. His parents were both dead, but his mother's brother was one of the baillies who sat on the council, a man with a rather high opinion of himself called Thomson. Now, James had ended up in the jail because of his love for music. He was an avid student of the violin and always eager to learn a new tune or improve his technique. So, when he reached his majority at the age of twenty-one and came into some money, he had devoted all of his time to music. His house became known to every passing fiddler as a place where you could always get food and drink and a bed, as long as you could teach the young lad something new. This, of course, led to many sessions in Jamie's house and he paid for everything. Although he had some money and the expectation of more down the years, he didn't have a great deal of ready cash. He certainly didn't have anywhere near enough to pay the vast bill he had run up with Laidlaw the grocer. And Laidlaw was a man who was known to pursue payment of bills like a hound from hell. He was also a baillie on the town council and a man who enforced his authority whenever he could. When Jamie couldn't settle up, despite having an uncle on the council alongside Laidlaw, the grocer insisted he be put in the debtors' jail. His personal possessions, including his fiddle, were confiscated by the grocer.

Jamie was despondent. If only he were free and had his fiddle again he would change his ways, he thought. He was so depressed, the thought that there would be more money from his father's estate in a few months was of no help.

Now, at this time prisoners relied on friends and family to keep them in food; there was precious little supplied by the town council and to supplement what they got they would street-fish. This was done by lowering a basket or bag out of one of the prison windows to the High Street below, in the hope of charity from passing strangers. Sometimes this might result in a loaf of bread or a few vegetables, but often enough mischievous laddies would put stones in the basket, bringing forth a stream of curses from the men in jail. Several of the others were trying their hand at this, but Jamie was too lethargic and depressed to join them; he was past caring.

Only a few days before, his uncle had taken great pleasure in telling him of a conversation he had had with Laidlaw.

'He asked me if I wasn't ashamed to hae my own sister's son in the debtors' jail for aw the town to see. He even said he would tak a monthly payment fae me till you get the next slice of your inheritance, in the spring, but I told him,' – and at this Thomson wagged his finger in his nephew's face – 'I told him straight: James is a grown man an every herring must hang by its own tail. He is of age an not my responsibility.' Normally, the smug look on his uncle's face would have infuriated Jamie, but he had been feeling too low to care.

There was a noise in the corridor outside and the jail door swung open to reveal Tippenny Torrance, the jailer, so-called for his well-known fondness for Tippenny or two penny ale.

'Hey, Fleming, ye hae a visitor. Get up,' he growled.

Behind him stood Baillie Thomson, with his peely-wally son William standing beside him.

'Weel, Jamie,' Thomson said, 'we won't let ye starve, though there's many who would, you ken. We have brought ye some boiled salmon, an make sure you keep it guarded from these miserable creatures in here.' He turned his head towards William and said, 'Look, William, what comes o a man who is not thrifty; James's mother must be turning in her grave. Well, hae you nothing to say, James?' Thomson stood there, smug and self-satisfied as ever, waiting for his nephew to crawl.

'Thank you, uncle,' murmured James, hardly caring at all, but noticing the smirk on Tippenny Torrance's coarse face as he stood beside the baillie.

'Right then,' said Thomson, 'let's go, William. We'll be back in a few days, James. Just ye think on your sins an pray to the Good Lord for guidance. Right, Torrance.'

The jailer opened the door and the three of them filed out.

To a few hungry looks from his fellow inmates, James unwrapped the paper parcel. In it there was a hunk of cold and greasy boiled salmon. He knew it came from Hungry Mary's filthy shop opposite the jail and was the cheapest foodstuff his uncle could get. He felt no hunger and the sight of the hunk of boiled fish turned his stomach.

'Here,' he said, turning to the man sitting a few feet to his right, 'you have it.'

This was McCrae, a man from Ross-shire, who had been thrown off the land his ancestors had worked for centuries to make way for the sheep that made his one-time clan chief rich. He had come to the town seeking work and had fallen on hard times, ended up here in the jail. He had hardly eaten for days. He gave Jamie a look of utter gratitude as he wolfed the fish down. Jamie lay back on the straw and drifted off into a half-sleep.

He lay half-dreaming on the straw, thinking back on long nights of fiddle-playing and good company, interspersed with blurred visions of the nearby mountains, where he had spent so many happy days. Suddenly he awoke with a start. The door was opening. This was unusual. Visitors usually came to the prison in the hours of daylight and it was dark outside. James looked up. There in the door stood his friend Jock Rose, and behind him were the figures of Fergie MacDougall, the surgeon's son, and Peter Wishart, whose father was a prosperous farmer and kept a house in the town. His three best friends. As ever, Jock, the madcap son of the senior baillie, was grinning broadly. He was known throughout the taverns and inns of the town as a lad who liked to have a good time and was always generous, and he and James had had many a grand night of fiddling and carousing.

James got to his feet as the three friends came into the jail, the looming figure of Tipenny Torrance behind them. The jailer looked worried.

'Now, come on, Master Rose, you can only stay a meenit,' he was saying.

'Ach, there's nae rule against visiting, is there now? Anyway, a man of your standing in the community can surely use his own discretion from time to time, don't you think?' said Jock over his shoulder. At that, James saw Peter slip something into the giant jailer's hand; the lumbering figure turned and left, pulling the door behind him but not locking it.

'Well, well, Jamesy boy,' said Jock, 'we thought you'd be getting a bit bored so we've come to cheer ye up. I'm sorry we cannae pay off your debts and get you out – we're a bit short for that, but we haven't come empty-handed.'

As James stood there bemused, looking at his friends, Fergie brought out two bottles of claret from under his coat, and Peter produced a bag of food.

'We've roast beef and half a chicken and some bread and potatoes here,' said Peter. 'We thought you might be a wee bit hungry.'

As the other prisoners looked on, the three friends sat down beside James and laid out their spread on a handkerchief spread on the straw. In truth, there was plenty of food and Jock said, 'There'll be enough for everybody to have a bite, I reckon.'

He was wearing a great black cloak and, as James tried to come to terms with what was happening, Jock spoke again.

'There's one more thing, Jamesie boy. I just managed to get my hands on this, at a price I must say, from that deil o a grocer.' And from under his cloak he brought out Jamie's beloved fiddle and bow.

James' face burst into a great smile and he reached out to take the precious instrument from his friend. 'Jock, Jock, what can I say?' he stuttered.

'Say?' cried Fergie. 'Say nothing. Just gie us a tune, you loon!' At that they all burst out laughing at the look of joy and confusion in their friend's face.

'We've spent all our cash,' put in Peter, 'but we can have a bit of a night in here for a change.'

'But first, James, just have yoursel a bite to eat an a drink,' said Jock.

But James could not wait. He felt as if he were dreaming as he raised his beloved fiddle to his chin then lifted his bow. He went straight into a spanking reel and his friends leapt to their feet and started dancing. The rest of the prisoners gave a cheer and James ripped through 'The Deil Amang the Tailors' with gusto. Stopping only to take a bite of a roast beef and a swig from a bottle held out to him by Fergie, James was off again. The food was passed around the jail's few occupants, followed by a bottle of claret; the three friends held onto the other one as they danced to Jamie's fiddle. He had only played one more tune, a rousing reel, when the door of the jail swung open. There stood Willie Webster, Torrance's apprentice, left in charge as his master went off to a nearby tavern with the money he had got from Peter. Webster looked in, gave a nod, and disappeared. He returned a few minutes later with his sweetheart, Jessie, the daughter of the jailer, coming in behind him.

191

In his ale shop, situated directly below the other jail room, Baillie MacIntosh was totting up his day's receipts when he heard what he thought was music. It was coming from the jail. Something was going on. Stopping only to knock on the door of the shop next door, a ships' chandlers owned by his close friend Allan Mowat, to ask the chandler to accompany him, he came up the stairs to the jail. He was followed by his wife and bairns, who had also heard the sounds in the house at the back of the shop. Mowat's wife and daughter weren't that far behind. Any break in the humdrum of small-town life was welcome and they were all interested to find out what exactly was happening. MacIntosh came to the unlocked door of the debtors' jail, pushed it open and stepped in. What a sight met his eyes! The jail was full of men dancing to the sound of the fiddle.

Drawing himself up to his full height of five feet five inches, Baillie MacIntosh put on his most serious-sounding voice and roared, 'What is going on here?' The music and dancing stopped.

From behind him his wife, who was a good couple of inches taller than her husband, said, 'Ach, dinnae fash, MacIntosh, they are just dancing, and why ever not? The lad is a grand fiddler. Get a grip on yerself, man.' At that, she turned to Jamie and asked, 'Do you know "Stewarton Lasses"?'

'It's one of my favourites, Mrs MacIntosh,' replied the fiddler, seeing which way the wind was blowing, and launched into the tune.

As he struck up, Mrs MacIntosh took her husband's hand and pulled him into the middle of the floor. Mowat, standing at the door, was a bit taken aback and muttered to his wife, 'This'll aw come tae a bad end.'

'Ach, wheesht, it's jist a bit o fun,' she replied and headed back downstairs to fetch her daughter. When she returned she showed all the practicality of the fairer sex, for she and her daughter were carrying candles, as well as a large jar of smelling salts to try and offset the rather pungent prison smell. Distributing both around the spartan room, they too joined in the festivities, pulling the recalcitrant Baillie Mowat with them.

During a wee break in the music, while the fiddler got his breath and had a glass of wine or two, there was a furious row from the other jail room across the corridor. The inmates there felt left out of things and were shouting to be allowed to join in. Just then, Tippenny Torrance came back upstairs and he roared at them to keep quiet. The chances of these thieves and vagabonds being allowed any licence was nil. However, by now Baillie MacIntosh was in the mood for a bit of fun and he sent one of his children downstairs to fetch some more drink. The festivities, and maybe the glass or three he had had himself, had loosened him up and he allowed a couple of flagons of ale to be handed through to the more serious criminals in the next room. In truth, they would have kept up such a noise they would have detracted from the enjoyment of all the others, so maybe it was just MacIntosh's basic practicality that won the day!

By this point, people in the street outside the jail had cottoned on to what was happening and word soon spread around the young folk of the town. One after another, young lads and lasses began to dance in the street below the jail. A few of them even sneaked upstairs into the jail, but there was hardly room for more than a handful of them. More drink was sent for and both Mrs Mowat and Mrs MacIntosh fetched food from their kitchens.

It was just turning nine as the provost and Baillie Laidlaw came round the town on their nightly perambulation. This was a part of their responsibilities they took seriously. Not only did it allow the baillies to keep an eye on what was happening around the town; it showed the citizens that these men of standing in the community took their responsibilities seriously indeed. While this activity made the pompous grocer feel even smugger than usual, the provost was a man who, though he took his responsibilities seriously, was sensible enough to know that keeping the towns-people happy was a good part of his job. In those days people were in their beds much earlier than is current practice; the nine o'clock walk around the town was seen by many as a clear suggestion that it was time to turn in.

They walked down the High Street. There in front of them was a group of couples dancing in the street. Shocked at the sight and paying no great attention to where the music was coming from, Baillie Laidlaw burst out, 'Never in my thirty years as a baillie have I seen anything like this . . . this is a scandal, provost. Hoi, you lot,' he shouted.

The dancers turned to see the provost and the baillie and, discretion as ever proving the better part of valour, the entire company disappeared as if by magic into the closes and vennels running off the High Street. Only then did the two men realise where the music was coming from. Laidlaw's face turned purple and it looked as if steam would come out of his ears. The one thing that was always said about Provost MacDonald was that he was quick on his feet, and even quicker with his brains.

'Now, now, Baillie Laidlaw, I'll tend to matters here. Just you get off home. I'll put a stop to this.'

Reluctantly, Laidlaw turned to go. He wanted to know what was going on but had spent his life sucking up to those of a higher station than himself – not that he saw it that way – and grunted assent before heading homeward.

The provost waited till the baillie was out of sight, then, there, alone in the High Street, he cut a few steps. In truth, he was a man who loved dancing but, what with the seriousness of his position, he tended to keep it quiet.

He sneaked into the jail and quietly went up the stairs. Looking carefully round the door of the debtors' jail, he saw the jailer, his assistant and two of the town's baillies amongst the dancers. He smiled to himself and disappeared back the way he had come. A short while later he went to bed singing to himself, an unusual occurrance in his household, and his wife awoke. Well, one thing led to another and the following morning the provost, and his wife, were in a very good mood over breakfast.

By the time the provost was drifting off to sleep, the party in the jail had been going for a few hours and the effects of the exercise and drink on the participants began to take its toll. In those days, of course, most people were up with the dawn and tended to follow the old adage of early to bed and early to rise.

Jamie himself was still fired up, but, as people began to drift away and others to sit on the floor of the jail, he started to play some of his favourite slow airs. This had the effect of a lullaby on some of those present. The two baillies and their families slipped out with smiles and nods to the fiddler, while two or three young couples stayed around a little while longer. Soon they too slipped away and no one was left apart from the prisoners, most of whom were themselves asleep, the two jailers, and Jamie's three pals.

One of the young couples had just turned in to their own street when they came across Baillie Rose, Jock's father. He had wakened in the night and, as so often before, had found his son was not in his bed – so he had gone out into the streets looking to find him in one of the taverns that sometimes stayed open into the small hours of the morning. The young couple had enjoyed the party in the jail and the lad could not resist temptation. 'Off to see your lad in the jail, eh, Baillie?' he quipped as they passed. Baillie Rose had no idea what he was talking about and muttered gruffly, 'Get home tae your beds; this is nae time for respectable people tae be out in the streets.'

Baillie Rose was awfully fond of his son but was in truth frightened that he could end up in jail like his friend the fiddler. He thought he heard some fiddle music – a beautiful old Gaelic tune he had often heard his mother sing in his youth – but he couldn't locate where it was coming from. The idea that it was coming from the jail never even crossed his mind.

A short while later, back at the jail, all was quiet. Jock, Fergie and Peter were all asleep on the straw in the debtors' jail. Webster and Torrance snored on the floor beside them. And the door stood open. Around the debtors' jail the prisoners lay sleeping soundly. All except one.

Just as dawn began to streak the sky, Torrance opened an eye. 'Och, heavens,' he said to himself, 'this willnae do at aw.'

He gave Webster a shove.

'Willie, waken up; we must get these laddies out o here quick.'

Half asleep, the assistant jailer helped Torrance shake the three visiting revellers awake and sent them home. People would soon be about the town and it would be better for all concerned if they woke up in their own beds. As Webster ushered them down the stairs, Torrance counted his prisoners. It was a habit of long standing.

There was one short, so he counted again, well aware that his brain was not functioning at its best. The same tally followed and he noticed that, amongst the scattered bottles and plates in the jail, there was no sign of the fiddle that had provided so much joy the night before.

Caught up in the sheer pleasure of having his fiddle back in his hands, Jamie had had much less to drink than anyone else there. Fired up with happiness at playing his beloved instrument, he was still wide awake when the last of his companions had fallen asleep. And there was the jail door wide open, just as it had been left by Baillie MacIntosh, who had stayed till near the end. Carefully stepping over the sleeping forms and clutching his fiddle, Jamie crept off down the stairs and out into the night.

As Torrance stood there, hardly wanting to think about the consequences of what had happened, Webster came back in. He too proceeded to count the prisoners, a habit he had picked up from the older man.

'Och, heavens, we're one short, Maister Torrance,' he squeaked.

'Aye, aye, it's young James himself,' replied the jailer, 'but maybe it's no quite as bad as it seems.'

'But, what do ye mean?' the younger man asked. 'We've let a prisoner escape; they'll probably lock us up ourselves.' His voice was getting higher and higher as panic surged through him.

'Naw, naw. There were twa baillies here last nicht and I doubt very much they'll want any noise made about this. I've been told more than one or two of the council were angry with Laidlaw for forcin young Jamie in here. An, though no awbody kens this, Provost Watson is a man that likes music. It's likely the only ane to be upset will be Laidlaw and that's no a bad thing. If necessary, the baillies will sort things out, even if it means dippin intae their own pockets. Well, no, I cannae exactly see any baillie doin that,' he went on. 'It's more likely that they'll pay off James' debts from the Common Good Fund, mark my words.'

The jailer's words were prophetic. James had gone off to stay with a cousin of his father's about twenty miles away, a place where he knew he would always be welcome, for wasn't he the one who had taught him the fiddle in the first place? Fergie knew this was where he was likely to head to and, when the council passed the motion settling James Fleming's debts, word was sent to the fiddler to come home. From then on he kept control of his natural generosity. It was no surprise to anyone when, a year or so later, he actually became the official town fiddler. Though Provost Watson always preferred that nothing was said of the night a fiddle unlocked the jail-house door.

Jack Broke the Prison Door

This is the title of a tune that was popular in Shetland fiddle circles. It is said to have been composed by a fiddler by the name of James Gaudie, who lived on the main island in the early years of the nineteenth century. Now, James was a physically big man who, because of an unfortunate accident in his youth, had developed a form of behaviour that led people to think him mad. While he was generally a gentle, even pious man, with a liking for theology, he could become a terror to the community when his fits came on him.

Even as a young lad he had shown an aptitude for playing the fiddle, as well as a tendency to bookishness, and was playing in public from an early age. Times were hard in Shetland then and, as he couldn't get enough gigs playing the fiddle, he went to work in a quarry when he was still in his early teens. Some say that it was here that he suffered the accident that was to blight the rest of his life – he was hit by a lump of falling rock – though there were rumours that he might have been assaulted by a jealous lover. Whatever the reason, while still a young man James began to suffer from bouts of recurring madness. His affliction consisted of little more than raging and shouting at people, but as he was such a big, fierce-looking lad this frightened quite a few of his fellow Shetlanders. His attacks came out of the blue and could last anything from a few hours to months at a time – months where he was almost impossible to control. It was understood by those who knew him that, although he became verbally abusive to all and sundry, he was no real threat to anybody.

Sometimes he could go for long periods, up to three years, without suffering one of his fits, though it seems that if he took strong drink that would set him off. He must have been all right much of the time, for he is said to have worked on the Greenland whaling in the early years of the century. This was hardly an easy life and it is unlikely that he could have lasted any time at all on a whaling ship if he had not been in total remission from his complaint. The one constant thing in his life, mad or sane, drunk or sober, was his fiddle. Whatever state he was in he would play as often as he got the chance. Musicians were always welcome on whaling ships for a variety of reasons. In the days before steam, the anchors had to hauled up and most of the heavy work associated with stripping whale carcasses had to be done by manual labour. This meant using the windlass, basically a massive hand-operated winch, and such work went better if it was done to a steady rhythm. What better for setting such a rhythm than a good tune or song? Many of the songs known as sea shanties derive from this and other activities which were carried out in groups. The other advantage of a fiddler or melodeon player was that, in case of overwintering, where a ship didn't get away from the far north before the ice set in, music was a great boon in the long dark hours of the Greenland winter. So Jamie might well have been paid extra as a musician when he was off whaling.

However, back in Shetland, on more than one occasion, he had to be taken into police custody because he was frightening people with his ranting. It also had an effect on his fiddling work; people were understandably a little cautious about hiring a fiddler who might fly off into an uncontrollable rage after having a few whiskies. In such situations it was pretty certain that he would be locked up. He would generally calm down after a few days and be released by the police. The local sergeant at the time, a man called Nicol, seems to have been relatively sympathetic towards the poor fiddler, though, given that Nicol was known to take a few glasses of the hard stuff himself, perhaps this wasn't all that surprising. He knew that, no matter how abusive James became, he could always be talked down. Leaving him in the prison till he returned to his normal placid character was the best way of dealing with the situation. Once he was in one of his fits, however, James had one peculiar habit that was certainly a bit destructive. Apart from shouting at anybody and everybody and terrifying children, he particularly liked breaking windows. Perhaps it was the crashing noise that attracted him. This was not a particularly serious offence, though anti-social. After one such occasion of window-breaking, Sergeant Nicol came and locked James up again. This time, however, he didn't calm down right away. In fact, he continued to be abusive to Nicol and the other policemen for several days and this came to the ears of the local magistrate. So when James was brought before him, the magistrate sentenced him to ten days in the jail. James had never before spent such a length of time behind bars.

After a week of this, James was totally recovered and he had his wits about him again. He considered that he had been badly done by and decided to rectify the situation by escaping from the jail. He barricaded the door of his cell with his bed; then, using the cutlery that had come with his evening meal, he dug the cement out from around the bars in his cell window. After that, it was easy enough for him to escape through the window. As he was no trouble when he wasn't having one of his fits, the police felt no need to keep a close eye on him and it was an hour or two before his escape was discovered. Later that same night he was picked up in a local hostelry, playing a new tune he had literally just composed, 'Jack Broke Down the Jail Door', to a selection of Lerwick's less salubrious citizens. They loved it and James was being wildly applauded when the police arrived. This seems to have been too much for the sergeant, who took personal offence at this flouting of authority, and his men dragged James away in irons.

He was brought up in front of the magistrate, a man who had seen him many times over the years. While the occasional bout of window-breaking and drunken rabble-rousing could be seen as little more than breach of the peace offences, this was something totally different. On hearing that the accused had had the temerity to go off to a tavern and compose a tune celebrating his own prison break, the magistrate decided enough was enough. Like many of his kind, he had a high opinion of himself and saw the fiddler's action as being an insufferable attack on the forces of law and order, and thus his own dignity. So he decided to have James sent off to a lunatic asylum. To make sure that there would be no chance of him ever getting out to trouble the upright citizens of Lerwick again, the magistrate ordered the unfortunate fiddler to be sent to the asylum in Morningside in Edinburgh.

At that distance, his family and friends would have little chance of trying to secure his release. Even trying to visit the unfortunate fiddler would be a major undertaking. The man chosen to accompany James was Sergeant Nicol himself. It seems that the sergeant's conscience perhaps got the better of him, for when he actually handed Gaudie over at the asylum it was noticed that he was drunk on duty. James himself was sober, but sadly spent the rest of his days within the asylum, though the tune he had composed continued to be a favourite in Shetland.

Military Matters

Members of the armed forces are like everybody else in their appreciation of music, and the power of music has always been understood by the military establishment, both on land and at sea. In this section we have a story of how a sailor won his way back on shore to play music in 'Over The Top', and a tale of how the fiddle can touch the hearts of the hardest of men in 'The Fiddler at Lucknow'.

Over The Top

Ayrshire has long been an area where Scottish culture has thrived. While the best-known Ayrshire man is undoubtedly the world-famous Robert Burns, there have been many fine musicians in Ayrshire since his time. One of these was Willie Carson, who was born in the 1830s near Dalbeattie. From an early age he showed a natural propensity for music and, with the encouragement and support of his parents, he became an adept fiddler in his early teens. As he grew through his teens, however, he grew a bit restless and wondered what the rest of the world beyond Ayrshire was like. Being a fit and adventurous young man, he decided to join the navy. Now, although serving in the navy had improved considerably in the previous few decades and was no longer as horrific, crude and miserable as it often was during the Napoleonic wars, it was still hardly a stroll in the park; living in cramped and smelly quarters, eating lousy (and often maggoty) food while working at hard physical labour was not really what had attracted

Willie to the navy in the first place. No doubt, he had dreamed of exotic journeys to sun-kissed islands populated by charming maidens or fighting in exciting battles in which he could show off his courage and skill. Instead, he ended up in a man-o-war patrolling off the African coast for three long years. Three years with few landfalls, rotten food and a mind-numbing monotonous repetition of the same thing every day in the hot and humid climate soon took the shine off his boyhood romanticism. The object of the patrol was to deter traders from other European countries coming into the British territories in West Africa, but the odd chase of a Spanish, Dutch or French trader only broke the monotony for a short time.

By the end of his third year Willie had decided that he had had enough. He wanted out. He could hardly afford to buy himself out with the pittance that was a seaman's wage, so he decided to try a trick that had been used by many a sailor before him. He would injure himself, just enough to be no longer of any use to the ship so would be sent home. We can only speculate as to his state of mind when he decided on his fateful action. Perhaps the monotony had resulted in what we now know can be a dangerous ailment indeed – depression. Perhaps he was completely at his wits' end and ready to try anything at all to escape. We do not know. What we do know is how he intended to 'work his ticket'. He got himself an axe and planned to cut off the tops of the fingers on his right hand, the hand with which he gripped his bow. What he had not counted on was that he would be carrying out this action with his left hand; he was right-handed.

So the day came when he was to do the deed. He gritted his teeth and swung the axe. Even though the fingers of his left hand were strong and dextrous from years of playing the fiddle, he was not used to handling tools with that hand. So his aim was not too good and, apart from chopping off most of his right-hand fingers, he took of a good bit of his thumb as well. His action had the required effect! Immediately after the 'accident' the wound was staunched with tar and, once the officers on board had seen what had happened, his passage home was guaranteed. Poor Willie though was in a state of fear and remorse. What if he could never grip his bow again? Would he ever be able to play his favourite tunes any more ? How could he hope to make a living if he couldn't play the fiddle? Luckily, once the wounds had scarred over, he found that he had just enough of his thumb and forefinger left for him to get a good grip on the 'scraper' with his right hand. His playing was in no real way diminished, once he got used to his new technique.

He returned to Ayrshire and, in a short space of time, had set himself up as a dancing master and fiddle teacher. He was successful from the very first and became well known around Dalbeattie. Willie possessed an understanding of all things mechanical and, even with his crippled right hand, he had a ready way with tools. These abilities, combined with his native intelligence, allowed him to do all sorts of musical-instrument repairs as well as carrying on with his chosen profession. His playing improved with time and he got the reputation of being a good and creative improviser. He also had a sense of humour; to lighten things up at various dances and performances he developed a remarkable party trick. He would fix a cello on a chair and, sitting on a raised chair alongside, would strap a bow to his left foot and proceed to vamp an accompaniment to his own violin on the cello! An early version of a one-man band.

The Fiddler at Lucknow

Throughout the history of the British Empire, wherever the fighting was hardest, you could be sure that at the front there would be a Scottish Highland regiment. Renowned throughout most of the world for their bravery and 'stickability', the kilted troops originally raised from the Highland clans in the eighteenth century were first-class soldiers. Some have said that they were seen as expendable by the government in Westminster, but so were the rest of the common soldiers of the British army. The Highland regiments, however, were all aware of their history and proud of their fearsome reputation. Wherever the action was the hottest, that was where they thought they should be. They saw action all over the world and often marched into battle with pipers playing stirring tunes at their head. The pipes were also a great source of comfort for the men off duty, reminding them of the distant hills of home and the loved ones waiting there. However, as the years passed and more and more of the men were recruited from the Lowlands, the fiddle began to assume a greater role for the soldiers in their off-duty hours. The pipes were still the official instrument of the Highland regiments, but for relaxation the fiddle was becoming much more common, its size and volume making it a bit more suitable for playing indoors anyway.

In 1857 what became known as the Indian Mutiny took place, with thousands of native soldiers (sepoys) turning against their colonial conquerors. While there were probably many Indians who wanted to get the British out of India, India itself had never been a single nation. The immediate trigger for the uprising had been the distribution amongst Muslim troops of rifle cartridges that were said to have been greased with pork fat. This was taken as blasphemy by the Muslim troops, who mutinied, with the result that there were many thousands of deaths on both sides. There were many bloody battles and sieges and, as ever, the Scottish Highland regiments were well to the fore. One particularly bloody campaign was the relief of Lucknow, which had been under siege by Indian troops for a considerable time. The battle was long and hard, but at last the British army was triumphant and the Indians were driven off.

The Highland Brigade under Sir Colin Campbell had played a major part in relieving the siege. They had taken many casualties and, in the Argyll and Sutherland Highlanders alone, six officers and men were eventually awarded the Victoria Cross, the British army's highest decoration, for their bravery in the battle. Afterwards, some of the troops were quartered in a requisitioned palace near another city some distance to the south to recuperate. Far from home in the searing temperatures of an Indian summer, many of the wounded, and others suffering from a variety of tropical diseases, would never see their homes again. One of the soldiers had gone into the city off duty and had managed to buy an old fiddle in the local market. With a bit of work, he soon had it ready to play and proceeded to perform a series of well-loved Scottish tunes. Later that same day he went to the wing of the palace being used as a hospital and played for his wounded and sick comrades. An hour or so after this, one of the officers was doing the rounds of the palace, checking on the watch guard. He could hear a slow air being played on the fiddle over in the hospital wing.

Up on a tower overlooking the hospital wing the officer came across a man he knew well. He was a twenty-year veteran corporal called Crawford, a man who had been exposed to all kinds of horror and danger. He had been cited in despatches on more than one occasion for his bravery and was currently up for a medal for his actions at Lucknow. To the officer's utter astonishment, Crawford was leaning on his rifle with his head down and tears pouring down his cheeks. The officer was aghast. Surely Crawford of all people was not cracking up? Certainly, they had been in a bloody battle and the conditions were pretty horrific but he had seen the man come through much worse with no ill-effect whatsoever. Unlike many of his class, the officer was a sympathetic man and had never held his men in contempt. Shell-shock was something unheard-of in those days, but he had seen enough to know that the horrors of war could sometimes drive men mad. But for Crawford to collapse like that – that was almost unthinkable.

He walked over to the soldier. 'Corporal, are you all right?' he asked.

Military Matters

At the sound of the officer's voice, the veteran soldier snapped to attention, hoisted his rifle over his shoulder, and saluted.

'Nothing to report, sir,' he said, but his attempt at barking out the response was muffled as he choked back his tears.

'Stand easy, man. Are you sure you're all right, Crawford? I can get someone to relieve you, if you are unwell,' the officer went on.

The grizzled veteran stood at ease, then turned and looked at him. The tears were clear to see all down his cheeks. 'Ach, sir, I'm fine. Dinnae worry yourself. It's just that auld Scottish fiddle tune, sir. It puts me in mind o the hills back hame an sae monie nights back on the croft by the fireside wi my father playin tae us. An there's an awfy lot o the lads down there will never get back to their own firesides.'

Then, giving himself a shake, he drew himself up to attention and said, 'Never mind, sir. I'll be fine. Though maybe you could ask that he plays a reel or two if ye're goin that way. I'm sure it would cheer a lot o us up.'

Blind Fiddlers

⇒•◦•⇐

Throughout human history in all parts of the world there have always been blind musicians. Music provided blind and partially-sighted people with a way of making a living, no matter how precarious. Here we have two stories – in the first the fiddler is totally blind, while Blind Alick MacDonald, in the second, is so called because his sight is so bad.

The Blind Fiddler and the Church Spire

Sandy McCrae from Kilmarnock was struck blind by smallpox as a child in the early years of the nineteenth century. However, he had already shown that he had a good ear for music and took to learning the fiddle with enthusiasm and commitment. By the time he was in his late teens he was very popular in the area around Kilmarnock and was getting plenty of work playing at the usual weddings and dances. In those days, many social celebrations were held in houses and farms all over the countryside and Sandy was often called out a fair distance from the town. In just few years he developed a remarkable skill. He only needed to be taken to a place once and then he could walk there and back unaided. Soon he knew virtually all the farmtouns for many miles all around. He had an unerring sense of direction and, walking at a steady even gait by the side of the road, he had even memorised stiles over hedges and knew where to take short-cuts across the corners of fields. This obviously took a great deal of concentration and Sandy was that rare thing among fiddlers of the time – a man who didn't take a dram! Of course, walking back from a gig in the dark was just the same to Sandy as walking there in daylight, so he always got back home safely – and if he had taken a drink that certainly would not have been guaranteed.

However, even if he didn't touch whisky, Sandy was no sourpuss. He was a man with both a sense of humour and a sense of adventure. One year, the new parish church at Riccarton was being built and Sandy got to hear of this. The church was being finished, with the scaffolding still surrounding the brand new spire, when our Sandy decided to bet that he could climb up to the spire and place a potato over the beak of the weather-cock on the top of the spire. He had an advantage over his friends in that the darker the night the more dangerous they thought it would be. But of course to Sandy it was all the same. So he had one friend let him know when a really dark night came and he headed off to the church with a group of his friends, some of whom were warmed up after a visit to the local howff. They were a bit worried; they had accepted Sandy's bet, but now, on this dark night with a strong wind blowing and the threat of heavy rain, they weren't sure at all that this was a good idea. They got to the foot of the scaffolding and some of them tried to call off the bet, but Sandy was having none of it.

'I've given my word and that's that,' he said.

By the light of a few flickering torches, Sandy started his climb. Soon he was out of sight in the gloom but he kept up a running commentary, with a few pretend gasps and slips, which only served to increase the worries of the crowd below. At last, however, he came to the top of the platform and, feeling for the beak of the weathercock with one hand, he took the potato from his pocket with the other and stuck it firmly, letting out a wild yelp of delight. Down below the gathered crowd thought it was a cry of fear and started shouting, 'Sandy, Sandy, are you all right?'

Several of them started climbing up the scaffolding themselves, but in the dark they were pretty helpless and were hardly off the ground when Sandy descended amongst them, laughing quietly to himself. There was great relief all round and there was no surprise in the morning when it was clearly seen that the brand new weather-cock had a large tattie stuck on its nose!

Blind Alick MacDonald

Alick MacDonald was born in Kirkoswald near Ayr in 1771. He was born with a serious eye defect and had trouble with his eyesight throughout his life. The problem caused him to wear very thick glasses and he was given the nickname Blind Alick at an early age. He was born into a family of weavers, but his deficient eyesight made it impossible for him to learn to be a weaver and he was encouraged to take up music. Luckily, he was born with a decent ear and the ability to carry a tune, and with some encouragement he soon showed himself to be a talented fiddler. At the age of nineteen he decided to leave his home in Kirkoswald and make his way in the world as a musician. Almost immediately, he ran into a colourful character who called himself Dr Hope and travelled the country selling quack medicines. In those days before the National Health Service, the services of doctors and necessary medicines had to be paid for and many of the poorer classes of society could not afford the cost, so there was a ready market for quacks like 'Doctor' Hope. The medicines sold at such travelling shows were often utterly useless and even the best of them might be little more than a strong laxative! However, there was little choice for most poor people in the growing industrial cities of Great Britain. When most people lived in the countryside, there were always a few old women who had knowledge of healing plants and herbs, experience in midwifery and some rudimentary bone-setting skills. Such women were much scarcer in the growing cities, though there were always howdies, or midwives, who often had some medical knowledge and skills. They were also the ones who laid out corpses for burial. But, other than that, there was little medical help for the poor and they were forced to rely on such dubious characters as Doctor Hope.

Hope needed a fiddler to help him drum up a crowd when he parked his caravan and set up his stall. Alick seemed to fit the bill. Tradition tells us that Alick would usually start with 'Rule Britannia', a tune that might not always meet with respect from Scottish city crowds, but one he liked. Alick was a strong supporter of the union with England and of the monarchy, and in modern terms would probably be seen as a Tory. He thought that he had landed himself a pretty good job and, on his very first night, he noticed a young lass in the crowd very near to the primitive stage he was playing at. She was paying close attention to the music and, when the time came to stop playing and let Doctor Hope begin his spiel about the remarkable virtues of the sublime tonic he was peddling, Alick stepped down off the stage and invited the young lady for a dram. Whether or not she was a beauty is impossible to say, but whatever she looked like she made a strong impression on Alick. Over a few drams in the tavern, Alick played her a few more tunes, something that gave her great pleasure and they both seemed to be very happy together.

So happy were they that not long after the two of them were married in the Whistlin Kirk on Glasgow Green, so-called because it was one of the first Scottish churches to install an organ, or 'kist o whistles', to accompany the singing. The church's old name is remembered to this day in the name of the pub there. Jessie continued to live with her parents near the Trongate in Glasgow and, as much of Alick's travelling with Doctor Hope was close to the city, he had plenty of opportunity to get back and see his new young wife. Life seemed pretty good to the young fiddler, but fate was about to intervene. Now, Alick might have been near blind but, as his skill with the bow clearly showed, he was not deaf. He soon began to realise that his playing was attracting considerable numbers of people and that Doctor Hope was doing an ever-increasing trade – a fact that made no difference to the wage he was being given. It seemed that Doctor Hope thought him a fool because of his bad eyesight and country origins. Possibly, however, given his way of making a living, the good doctor was simply not overly concerned with honesty.

Alick broached the matter one night in Coatbridge. 'We seem to have done very well tonight,' he said to his employer.

'Ach, fair, just fair, Alick,' came the reply.

'Well, I was listening and it seems to me that you sold about 150 bottles of the tonic tonight,' Alick said forcefully.

'Ach, no, no, no, it was more like a hundred; ye see, I hae it marked down here.' Hope held up a piece of paper covered with small neat handwriting and a lot of numbers. He knew fine well that in the deepening gloom of the evening his fiddler would be unable to make out anything on the paper at all.

'Well, is that so? I cannae see too well but you are playin me for a fool, Hope,' Alick insisted. 'You said I would be on a share of the takins; over the past few weeks I have been takkin notice o just how many bottles you've been sellin, and you have never given me any more than I was gettin at the start.'

'Are ye callin me a cheat, ye blind guttersnipe?' The Doctor pulled himself up to his full height, about four inches shorter than the fiddler, hoping to face him down.

'I never said you were a cheat but you brought it up. I maybe cannae see but I can count and, by my reckonin, you owe me fifteen shillins.' Then he grabbed Hope by the front of his shirt and shoved his face so close that his glasses were up against the quack's nose.

'Fifteen shillins! You're jokin . . .' Hope began, but, as the fiddler's grip tightened, he realised that he was caught. The upshot was that Alick got his fifteen shillings, a fair sum back in the 1890s, but his employment was terminated by mutual consent. He didn't want to work for a cheat and a thief. Hope was furious that this blind whippersnapper from the country had turned out to be a lot smarter that he thought. Alick headed back to see his wife in the city, his pockets jingling, and within a day or two had begun playing in the streets around the Trongate. He was already known to a few people from his work with Hope, but his skill as a fiddler soon began to draw crowds. Pretty soon, he and Jessie had their own wee tenement flat near the Trongate.

Although Alick had extremely bad eyesight, he had learned to read as a child and he had discovered that he had a facility for words. He was in no way the fool that Hope had thought him. Over the next few years he began to intersperse his fiddle-playing with occasional bursts of rhyme; it was hardly poetry, and was exclusively concerned with the news of the day, but, like the work of that other nineteenth-century rhymester, William McGonagall of Dundee, his words were direct and accessible and popular with his audience, the common people of Glasgow. This increased his earning power in the streets. He would play for a while till a crowd gathered, then give them the news in rhyme. Jessie would take a collection, and then they would move on to another spot and repeat the process. Soon he was a weel-kennt figure around the Trongate and people looked forward to his daily appearances on the streets. His penchant for reciting the news was soon to find a new subject.

In January 1793 the new revolutionary government in France executed their king, Louis XVI, and Britain declared war on the French. As a fervent royalist, Blind Alick was a hundred per cent behind the declaration of war. Other Scots of the period were initially supporters of the French movement towards liberty, equality and fraternity. Rabbie Burns, working as an exciseman for the government, had even gone so far as to send a couple of carronades, or small cannon, to the revolutionary government in Paris – they were intercepted at the English Channel – and throughout Scotland those people hoping for democratic reform initially saw the developments in France as helpful to their cause. The execution of the king changed many minds, but throughout much of the 1790s the movement for democratic reform in Scotland, Ireland and England continued to thrive. The response of the government in Whitehall was typically unimaginative and brutal. In Scotland, a group of men, since known as the Political Martyrs, were transported to Botany Bay in Australia for daring to agitate for political reform – reform which had been the avowed intent of the British prime minister, William Pitt, only a few years earlier. The attitude of the government can be plainly seen in the transportation of the Political Martyrs – transportation had never been incorporated as a punishment into Scots Law. Alick, however, had no doubt about where his loyalties lay. He was for king and country.

He took great pleasure in giving out his newscasts as the war developed. In fact, he went further: between his fiddling he regularly performed verses in praise and support of the regiments that were raised in Glasgow to fight the French. His support for the Glasgow Volunteers and the Glasgow Sharpshooters was warmly greeted by many, but there were those who realised that the government was using the battle with the French as an excuse for repression at home. Most people, however, rallied to support the government during the war and Alick prospered. In fact, he made so much money that he paid for several operations to try and correct his defective eyesight. Ophthalmology in those days was still relatively undeveloped and, despite his expenditure, his eyesight failed to improve – in fact, the operations made his eyesight even worse. Still, he continued to prosper and by the time the war was over in 1802 he was quite comfortable.

Alick continued to ply his trade as a fiddler and embryonic newscaster around the Trongate area for many more years. The wars with Napoleon gave him many opportunities to sing the praises of the British army, and its Glasgow regiments, as he gave out the news. When Napoleon escaped from Elba and returned to France to raise another army in 1815, Alick was out there on the streets stirring up patriotic support for the army. And when the news of Waterloo finally came through he had the greatest opportunity of his life. By now well-versed in getting new information as quickly as the publishers of the newspapers, he could get the news out hours before the printers could get the papers on the streets. People flocked to hear him chant his rhymes about the final defeat of Bonaparte, interspersed with rousing patriotic tunes on the fiddle. People cheered and clapped as he gave his version of the great British victory – the relief at war being over and the hoped-for return of loved ones serving in the forces was widespread. Alick was in his element and the money poured in. The euphoria lasted for a good few weeks, but all things must pass.

Alick's adherence to king and government began to lose its attraction in the years after the defeat of Napoleon. Back in the 1790s there had been direct repression by the government in response to outbreaks of dissent all over the Highlands and Lowlands, with protestors being killed in such a seemingly unlikely location as Tranent in East Lothian. But by 1820 there was even more widespread demand for change. Soldiers and sailors returning home found there were few jobs; vast sections of the populace were living in poverty. By 1820, when the weavers of Lanarkshire were lured into an ambush by the British army in an episode known ever since as the Rising, popular opinion was hardening in favour of reform. The show trials of so-called rebels and the hanging of an inoffensive weaver called Purley Wilson from Strathaven, guilty of nothing more than wanting to make life better for his family, were hardly going to make the approach of government popular, especially as agents provocateur had been active in stirring up the weavers. The Great Reform Act of 1832 was still a long way off, but the writing was on the wall. The old corrupt practices of the British government could no longer be hidden and the public's acceptance of repression and the suppression of dissent were exhausted, particularly after the slaughter at Peterloo in Manchester in 1819.

The dissent reached right to Alick's door. The weavers of Calton rioted and Alick's old favourites, the Glasgow Sharpshooters, marched into the Gallowgate barracks. The weavers barricaded themselves in Anderston and Calton and the Sharpshooters were sent in to clear the streets. Houses were searched for supposed caches of weapons and many weavers were arrested, none too gently; the whole area was sacked. Popular feeling against the soldiers ran high. Never again would Alick manage to run with the stream of pubic opinion and when, as an old man, he played his fiddle in the streets around the Trongate people remembered that he had been a notable public figure, but most of them couldn't be sure exactly for what. His devotion to king and country was outdated when all around him perceived only the corruption and intransigence of an organisation in need of a major overhaul. So he ended up as nothing more than a street fiddler, like so many others in Glasgow. In his career, though, he had seen the highs and lows, and for a while had been at the very centre of events in the growing commercial centre of the empire's second city. The stirring towards reform that he had been unable to comprehend eventually resulted in widespread democratic reform in the 1830s, too late for Blind Alick, who passed away in 1830.

The Fiddling Tradition

⊰◈⊱

This group of stories brings together some tales of Scotland's fiddling history – and a famous poem.

Fiddlers' Close

Back in the 1830s and '40s Glasgow was a growing city. The move from the land to the towns was well under way as thousands of cottars were cleared from the Lowlands of Scotland to make way for 'improved' agriculture. In the Highlands, the better-known clearances were also under way; landowners began moving thousands of people off the land and away from a way of life that had been the same for generations. Men who had once been the chiefs of clans made up of their own relations were now no more than money-grubbing landlords, looking to fill their pockets any way they could in the name of progress. The shift to a city-based economic society threw many people into poverty. Jobs were hard to find for many cleared people, but one way some of them could earn a crust was as street musicians. There were many people who had jobs in the cities, particularly in a thriving port and mercantile centre like Glasgow, and music, especially fiddle-music, was always appreciated at all levels of society. So there were hundreds of street fiddlers. Many of them barely scraped a living and were in need of cheap – extremely cheap – digs. These were generally found at a filthy old tenement in the High Street, to which they gave their name. For only a few pence the poverty-stricken street fiddlers could stay in the high building at Fiddlers' Close, above a howff, or tavern, that many of them frequented. Like the doss-house above, this smoke-blackened and battered old hostelry was known for one thing above all. It was cheap! And in the lodgings themselves were many street players whose sole bed was the broad of their back upon the plain wooden boards of the floor. Those of them fortunate to have fiddle cases – it was still the practice for many of them to carry their fiddles in a velvet bag, just as Niel Gow had done – could use their cases as pillows.

Fiddler Poets

———⟫◆⟨———

Two of Scotland's finest poets are known to have played the fiddle: Robert Burns and James Hogg. Both of them were keen songsmiths and steeped in their respective local traditions. While neither of them was a virtuoso, they seem both to have been very fond of fiddle music. This is hardly surprising as it was the most popular musical instrument in Scotland throughout both their lives, Burns being born in 1759 and Hogg dying in 1835. Burns' sister wrote that he started learning the fiddle in 1781 and that in the winter, when he was first up to light the fire, he would often play for the rest of the family still lying in their beds. Burns met Niel Gow in 1787 and, as an avid collector of songs and tunes, there is little doubt that he must have enjoyed the fiddler's company. Perhaps their conversation turned to other things; there are rumours that Gow 'was out' in the '45 for a while and Burns had a great interest in Scottish history and politics. What is certain is that both men had a disdain for people who were full of 'airs and graces'. Neither of them was in any awe of their supposed social betters and, while we can be sure that Burns was of a radical disposition – his 'A Man's a Man' is probably the world's greatest anthem to equality – Gow's common-sense attitude to his fellow man was probably some-what less intellectual than the poet's.

Burns's genius allowed him to create the fascinating 'The Deil's Awa Wi the Exciseman', in which the devil is presented as playing the fiddle and ensnaring the exciseman in a Pied Piper of Hamlin fashion. The poem is a snapshot of Scottish culture in its language, music, and the themes of dancing, drinking and avoiding tax on alcohol!

The Deil cam fiddlin thru the toun
An danced awa wi the Exciseman
An ilka wife cries, 'Auld Mahoon,
I wish ye luck o the prize, man.'

Chorus
The Deil's awa, the Deil's Awa
The Deil's awa wi the Exciseman
He's danced awa, he's danced awa
He's danced awa wi the Exciseman.

We'll mak our maut, an we'll brew our drink
We'll laugh, sing an rejoice, man
An monie braw thanks tae the muckle black Deil
That danced awa wi the Exciseman.

Chorus

There's threesome reels an foursome reels
There's hornpipes an Strathspeys, man
But the ae best dance that eer cam tae the land
Was the Deil's awa wi the Exciseman.

Here Burns presents the devil as 'fiddlin thro the toun', reflecting the widespread belief that the devil played the fiddle for witches' covens; in 'Tam o Shanter' he had Auld Hornie playing the pipes for Cutty Sark and her pals. The song reflects the widespread dislike of excisemen or 'gaugers' as they were known, and the fact that Burns himself served as an exciseman gives an extra edge to the satire. Fiddles turn up in various of Burns' works like 'The Jolly Beggars'.

Reflecting his accuracy as social commentator, he also wrote an epitaph for Andrew Jamieson of Lockerbie that goes:

> Oh sirs, but it is sad that death aye reaves us
> O aw the guid anes, an the ill anes leaves us
> Were there naw Cowdans, Urines an sic snools
> But Andrew's black head maun grace the mools.

The reference to Cowdans and Urines (Irvines) is to local fiddle-players whose skills were considerably less than Jamieson's. Snools are spiritless, cringing fellows and Andrew's head graced the mools, the earth, because he was buried therein. Burns' well-known 'Rattlin Roarin Willie' refers to Willie Dunbar, a member of the Edinburgh social club called the Crochallan Fencibles, in whose company the poet spent many convivial hours. The song was perhaps suggested by an earlier song about another Rattlin Willie, whose story has been told here.

In the poem 'Epistle to Davie', to his publisher Thomson, a fellow fiddler, Burns wrote:

> Hale be your heart, hale be your fiddle!
> Lang may yer elbuck jink and diddle,
> To cheer you thro the weary widdle
> O warldy cares,
> Till bairns' bairns kindly cuddle
> Your auld gray hairs.

Thomson published six volumes of the melodies of Scotland (*The Scots Musical Museum*), helping to preserve some of the tunes to Burns' collection of songs – some written by him, some traditional songs – which remain popular all over the world to this day.

Hogg is thought to have been a bit more of a fiddler than Burns; it is said that he used to entertain the cows on his father's farm as he practised in his bedroom above the byre. He got his first fiddle at fourteen and went on to write 'Charlie is my Darlin' and 'Come Oer the Stream, Charlie', reflecting the influence of the romantic notions of the Jacobite rebellions that coloured the atmosphere in late eighteenth- and early nineteenth-century Scotland. Like Burns in Ayrshire, he was steeped in the traditional culture of the Scottish Borders, his mother in particular being a real tradition-bearer with a host of ballads and songs committed to memory. Hogg himself wrote many poems in the style of the old Border Ballads, one of the most important song traditions in the world. At the age of fourteen he saved five shillings from his wages and bought an old fiddle, teaching himself to play it in the evenings when his day's work was done, and going on to play at various fairs in the area. He was virtually illiterate until the age of eighteen, when he became a shepherd and was lent books and newspapers by his employers, especially by James Laidlaw of Blackhouse farm, whom he served for ten years from 1790, and whose kindness he later described as 'much more like that of a father than a master'. Like Burns, he was a great collector of traditional songs and there can be little doubt that both of them were capable of sympathetic understanding of their own national music traditions through their knowledge of the fiddle. In playing the fiddle they were both participants in a living tradition which they, in turn, helped so much to popularise throughout the world.

The Fiddler's Widow

—➤◆◆⤛—

A poem by Andrew Scott (1751–1839)

There was a musician wha played a good stick
He had a sweet wife and a fiddle
An in his profession he had richt good luck
At bridals his elbow to diddle

But Ah! The poor fiddler soon chanced to die
As aw men to dust must return
An the poor widow cried wi her heart an her ee
That as lang as she lived she would mourn

Alane by the hearth she disconsolate sat
Lamenting the day that she saw
An aye as she looked on the fiddle she grat
That silent nou hung on the wa

Fair shone the red rose on the young widow's cheek
So newly weel washen wi tears
An in cam a younker some comfort to speak
Who whisper'd fond love in her ears

Dear lassie, he cried, I am smit with your charms
Consent to marry me now
I'm as good as ever laid hair upon thairms
An I'll cheer baith the fiddle an you

The young widow blush'd but sweet smiling she said
Dear sir to dissemble I hate
If we twa together are doom'd tae be wed
Faith we neednae contend agin fate

He took down the fiddle, so dowie it hung
An put aw the thairms in tune
The young wife dighted her cheeks an she sung
For her heart lap her sorrow aboun

And now sleeps the dead in his cold bed o clay
For death still the dearest maun sever
For now he's forgot an his widow's fou gay
An his fiddle's as merry as ever.

Grat: cried; *younker*: young man; *thairms*: strings; *dowie*: sad;
dighted: wiped; *lap*: leapt; *aboun*: above; *fou gay*: very happy.

The Fiddlemaker and
the Hidden Fiddle

⟫⟨

S ome traditional instruments have always been home-made
and, as we have seen, there were several players who turned
their hands to making fiddles in Scotland. The creation of simple
box-fiddles and kits perhaps did not require great skill but, with
the increasing sophistication of violin-making techniques from
the seventeenth century onwards, musicians increasingly wanted
high-quality instruments made by specialist violin makers. Of all
the Scottish fiddle-makers the best is generally accepted to have
been Matthew Hardie, and here is a story about him.

The making of violins and fiddles is more of an art than a craft.
Although the sixteenth-century Italian masters such as Stradivarius
and Guarnerius are recognised throughout the world as the
greatest, Scotland had its own share of master craftsmen who
could make wonderful, sweet-sounding and long-lasting instruments. Probably the most famous of these was Matthew Hardie,
who was born in Edinburgh in 1755. He probably trained initially
as a cabinet-maker but was lucky to find a local violin-maker,
John Blair, who showed him the ropes. So successful was Hardie
as a violin-maker that Blair ended up working for him. In the
second half of the eighteenth century the fiddle was far and away
the most popular musical instrument in Scotland. Hardie did a
good a steady trade from his shop in the Low Calton, below what
is now the Regent Bridge in Waterloo Place at the east end of

Princes Street. Although there have been rumours that Hardie was very fond of whisky, there seem little grounds for thinking it affected his production of violins and cellos, for which there was also a steady demand as an accompanying instrument for the fiddle at dances and balls. Such was his skill at making violins that Hardie found himself at various times teaching a range of other fiddle-makers how to improve their skills. He was in time succeeded by his son, who sadly never managed to make instruments of as fine a quality as his father. Hardie is generally accepted as the finest of the Scottish fiddle-makers and his instruments are still sought-after to this day.

Like all other artists, Hardie always had his eye out for suitable wood for making fiddles. One day in 1821 he was out for a walk with a friend on the Cramond Road when he saw a piece of wood lying at the edge of a field. It was an old weather-beaten paling-slab. Picking it up and holding it on the ends of his fingers, he found a piece of stone and struck the wood with it. The sound that came off pleased him and he turned to his companion and said, 'I think I have a fiddle breast here, and a good one too.'

They walked on and a short while later stopped at a farm house to see if they could get a glass of milk. The farmwife was pleased to oblige and led them into the kitchen to give them their drinks. While drinking his milk, Hardie looked around the kitchen. There, sitting on a dresser, was an old baking board made of maple. 'I can see, mistress, that you have a very fine fiddle in the house,' he said, with a smile.

The farmwife was taken aback. 'Och, there never was such a thing in this hoose,' she said, a bit flustered.

'Oh, but there is,' replied Hardie, 'though I have to admit it's gey well-hidden. Still, though, I would like to buy it from you.'

'If you can find a fiddle hereabouts, sir, ye're welcome tae tak it with ye, for nothing at all,' came the reply.

At that, Hardie took the baking board into his hands and turned to speak to the woman.

'I thank you very much indeed. The fiddle is in this baking board and I can hear it crying to get out. So I'll take you at your word. I have the breast of the same fiddle with me already,' he went on, showing her the paling. 'I must away and start to put the instrument together.'

With that, he and his friend left, but the following day the woman was pleased to take delivery of a brand new baking board. So both ended up satisfied with the bargain. Hardie always said that this was the origin of one of the best fiddles he had ever made. I have heard that this self-same fiddle ended up in the hands of Ian Powrie, leader one of Scotland's best-kennt country dance bands.

And Finally . . .

The Fiddler's Deathbed

In Victorian times people had what we would now see as a peculiar attitude towards death. It seems as if they were absolutely fascinated with the subject and the sentimentality of the times seems to us quite extreme. An example of this was the popularity of deathbed paintings and there is one that was particularly well-liked. This was 'The Fiddler's Deathbed' by W. Dobdon. This was said to have been painted from real life. James Whyte was the porter for forty years at the railway station in Dunblane. In 1888 he was on his deathbed and sent for John Rodgers, a man as old as himself, who had regularly played for the passengers at the station for thirty years and more, and asked him to play 'The Land o the Leal' at his bedside as he passed away. Dobdon's painting of the scene proved very popular and many prints of the painting were sold.

There is a story of a fiddler that supports just such a sentimental way of looking at things. William Marshall was born at Fochabers in 1748 and started his working life as a gardener at Gordon Castle in Huntly. Although he never had much formal schooling, Marshall went on to become a fine fiddler and an extremely prolific composer. There were those in the nineteenth century who thought that his collections of fiddle tunes were second to none. Perhaps it was his great musical skill that brought him to the attention of the duke of Gordon, for he became house steward and then butler to the duke. In 1790 he took over a farm at Keithmore and combined the running of the farm with the role of the duke's factor. As if this wasn't enough to keep him busy, he carried on composing at a steady rate as well as playing the fiddle at every event he could. He composed the music for the song 'Of Aw the Airts the Wind can Blaw', which was a great favourite in his lifetime, as well as many other tunes that found a ready audience. Like many another man of his time, despite his farming and fiddle interests, he found time to become an accomplished dancer and was a great lover of fishing and hunting. He clearly had an active mind as he also took to building clocks, some of which were very complicated indeed. In short, he was a man of great talents and frightening energy, whose reputation amongst his fellow musicians was considerable. When at last, in the fullness of his years, he took to his bed for the last time at the fine old age of eighty-five, he had a full and happy life to look back on.

When he realised that death was approaching he sent for the minister at nearby Elchies. This was hardly surprising at a time when most Scots were deeply religious, but William had something else in mind other than praying and getting ready to face judgement. He knew the minister well and they had often spent convivial evenings playing together, for the minister was a practised fiddler and had learned a great many of Marshall's compositions. When the minister arrived he had Charles Grant, the local dominie (schoolteacher), with him, another fine fiddle-player and one-time pupil of Marshall's. They knew pretty much what to expect and Marshall's last hours were spent listening to his own tunes being played to him by the minister and the dominie. And the word is that he surely died with a smile on his face.